EARLY TRAMWAYS
~IN~
Yorkshire
A Golden Age

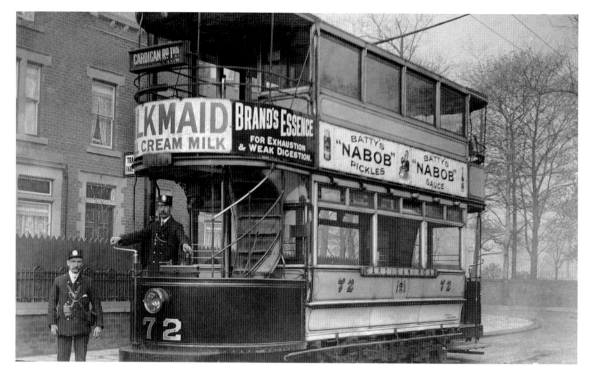

Leeds, Cardigan Road

Leeds Corporation's double deck, top covered, open balcony car no. 72, displaying a Cardigan Road route board, was built by Brush Electrical Engineering Co. Ltd, of Loughborough (Brush) and entered service on 13 October 1904. A vestibule was fitted on 13 January 1913 and withdrawal came on 9 February 1939.

Bradford, Bailiff Bridge

In some instances Bradford Corporation took the fleet numbers of withdrawn vehicles and allocated them to other ones. For example, no. 119 was allocated three times. The 'second' car no. 119 - a double deck, top covered, open balcony, vestibule vehicle - is seen at Bailiff Bridge after 1919 when route numbers were introduced - 13 being Bailiff Bridge.

EARLY TRAMWAYS

~IN~

Yorkshire

A Golden Age

PETER TUFFREY

FONTHILL

Sheffield, Crookes terminus

Sheffield Corporation's double deck, open top car no. 235, built by Brush in 1904, is at the School Road Crookes terminus. The electric tramway route opened from Crookes Junction to Lydgate Lane on 1 April, 1901. It was extended to School Road, 18 April 1902 and to Heavygate Road 26 November, 1913. Trams ceased to run to Crookes on 4 May, 1957. Interestingly, by March 1904, Sheffield had 237 vehicles in service. They had run 5,768,231 miles with traffic receipts of £232,351. The total number of trams in service in Great Britain at that time was 6,783.

Fonthill Media Limited
Fonthill Media LLC
www.fonthillmedia.com
office@fonthillmedia.com

First published 2014

ISBN 978-1-78155-349-7

Printed in England

Contents

Leeds, Briggate

On the left, in Briggate, Leeds, a Kitson & Company, Leeds (Kitsons) engine is hauling a converted single deck trailer car. In the foreground, a steam engine built by Thomas Green & Son Ltd, Leeds (Greens) is coupled to double deck trailer car no. 36 constructed by Geo.F. Milnes & Co, Birkenhead (Milnes).

Acknowledgements

I am grateful for the help received from the following people: Paul Bolton, David Clay, Norman Ellis, Hugh Parkin, Jane Salt, Alan Sutton.
Special thanks are due to my son Tristram for his help and encouragement throughout the project.

Photographs

Every effort has been made to gain permission to use the photographs in this book. If you feel you have not been contacted please let me know: petertuffrey@rocketmail.com.

Information

I have taken reasonable steps to verify the accuracy of the information in this book but it may contain errors or omissions. Any information that may be of assistance to rectify any problems will be gratefully received. Please contact me by email petertuffrey@ rocketmail.com or in writing Peter Tuffrey, 8 Wrightson Avenue, Warmsworth, Doncaster, South Yorkshire, DN4 9QL.

Introduction

I am a proud Yorkshireman with a deep passion for old trams and after locating a massive postcard collection depicting them in a variety of street scenes around the region, I could not help myself producing this book. It is also noted that a number of significant developments in the history of tramways took place in Yorkshire and these will be mentioned in due course. And I must thank Fonthill MD Alan Sutton, once more, for supporting the project.

I am also fortunate that many of the illustrations capture the opening days of a system or early years of horse or steam tramway operations. Thus the book covers the period roughly from the 1870s to around 1925 - to some the Golden Age of tramways. It is a period where Yorkshire cities and towns attempted to get to grips with transporting people around their localities particularly when the region as a whole saw massive developments in the steel, coal and woollen industries.

Street tramways had originated in the United States, and were introduced to Britain by George Francis Train in the 1860s. The first recorded installation was a short line from Woodside Ferry to Birkenhead Park in the town of Birkenhead. Yet, when Train started laying lines on top of the highway in London, he was arrested and fined - even though he argued he thought he had obtained permission.

To anticipate and regulate a perceived boom in tramways across the country, the Tramways Act of 1870 was passed. Its purpose was to promote new tramways by clarifying and regulating the legal position. Under the act local boroughs or urban district councils could grant a 21-year concession to a private tramway operator. Operators could construct the track as part of the concession but were responsible for the repair of the public highway between the tracks and a short distance either side. The local authority could construct the track themselves if they wished to retain complete control of the highway, but they were not allowed to operate trams. At the conclusion of the lease, the local authority could purchase the complete undertaking, including the trams, steam engines and horses. Several sections of the Act were later repealed or superseded by other legislation. Under newer Acts, including the Light Railways Act 1896, local authorities were given the right to construct and operate their own tramways, and municipal ownership became the norm when the original concessions expired.

Many Yorkshire cities and towns followed the pattern of tramway developments that were mirrored across the UK. Usually, an approach was made by a company to a local authority and after much wrangling about costs and responsibilities a horse tramway, in most cases, was established.

For example, Bradford Corporation gained Parliamentary approval under the Bradford Corporation Tramways Order, 1881 to construct its own tramway system within the city.

It was then leased to the Bradford Tramways Company (later the Bradford Tramways and Omnibus Company Limited).

The Dewsbury, Batley & Birstal Tramway Company (DB&BTC) was a tramway pioneer, completing the first British on-street system in 1875 between Dewsbury and Birstall in 1875.

Although horse trams were still a crude means of transport it was often said it was an improvement on horse omnibuses. The low rolling resistance of metal wheels on iron or steel rails, allowed the animals to haul a greater load for a given effort than the omnibus and gave a smoother ride. The horse-drawn streetcar combined the low cost, flexibility, and safety of animal power with the efficiency, smoothness, and all-weather capability of a rail right-of-way.

Near the end of the century, steam trams coupled to trailers began to appear in areas, most notably in Leeds where for a few years they enjoyed moderate success. By contrast, in York they were abandoned after complaints about noise and dirt. Yet, Huddersfield Corporation opened its first steam tram route - between Lockwood (Red Lion Hotel) and Fartown (Royal Hotel) - on Thursday 11 January, 1883, becoming, as stated by Brook (1959) the first U.K. municipally-operated tramway system.

In time, horse and steam trams gave way to electric trams, and the Roundhay Electric Tramway (RET), in Leeds, according to Soper (1985) was 'the first to be operated by an overhead wire system in Europe, and which was formally opened on Thursday, 29 October 1891.'

Of course, the opening of a new electric tramway route was a great occasion in many areas of Yorkshire and indeed the rest of the country, and brought out children and adults alike to witness the event. All of this was thankfully recorded by the armies of postcard photographers whose trade was also new and booming at the same time as electric trams.

A strange diversion from the overhead electric system was the one that used Dolter surface contact studs. Introduced by the Mexborough & Swinton Tramways Company in 1907, at a cost of £14,000, it was abandoned a year later because of a series of recurring incidents. These included loud bangs and flames beneath the cars, fatal electric shocks to horses, and trams being marooned and having to be pushed along the road by passengers to regain electric power.

The brief interlude with trolleybuses, but more importantly the advent of personal motor vehicles and the improvements in motorised buses, led to the rapid disappearance of electric trams. Sheffield became the last city in Yorkshire and England operating trams, closing on Saturday afternoon 8 October 1960. Glasgow (Scotland) was the last in the UK, closing in 1962.

CHAPTER 1
East Yorkshire

Hull

Hull Trams The Early Days (1977) explains that the Continental & General Tramways Company was authorised to construct horse drawn tramways in Hull during the early 1870s. But, 'after the opening of the first line - the Beverley Road route - [on 9 January 1875] the Continental & General Tramways Company was authorised to sell its interests to the Hull Street Tramways Company,' states the book. The sale was sanctioned at a meeting of the shareholders of the Hull Street Tramways Company on 16 October, 1876. On the first day of operation on the Beverley Road route, it is recorded that 1,116 passengers were carried. A half hourly service was provided by two trams which were hauled by Flemish horses. The first official licensed drivers and conductor of street tramways in Hull were: Charles Sissons and William Jackson (drivers) and Edward Read (conductor). The Hull Street Tramways Company obtained powers under the Hull Street Tramways Act 1875 to complete the partly constructed tramways started by the Continental & General Tramways Company. Thus, further routes were opened, including the Hessle Road branch, on 7 April 1877; the Anlaby Road route shortly after a trial run on 25 May 1877 and a service between Spring Bank and the Pier in February, 1878. A service to Holderness Road also commenced. By this time there were seven miles of track and over 31,500 passengers were being carried each week. Four years later it was recorded that the Hull Street Tramways Company owned 121 horses and 25 trams. There were three company depots, on Hessle Road (near Regent Street), Temple Street, and at Jesmond Gardens. The picture shows double deck horse car no. 23 at the Temple Street (Beverley Road) depot.

In 1889 a route along Hedon Road was served by steam trams of the Drypool & Marfleet Steam Tramways Co. Hull Corporation acquired the Hull Street Tramways Company in May 1895 for £12,500. In the following year the Corporation accepted a tender from a Mr Nettleton to operate the horse trams for a period of a year at a time. The Corporation completed the purchase of the Drypool & Marfleet Steam Tramways Company, agreed at a price of £15,500 in 1894, but not completed until October 1899. Illustrated is a steam car and trailer on Hedon Road c. 1896.

On Thursday 9 June 1898, the official ceremony of laying the first Hull Corporation electric tramway rail took place in Porter Street and was attended by Works Committee Chairman Alderman Larard. Siemens supplied the electrical equipment, the rails, 4ft 8½in. gauge, from Société Anonyme des Aciéries d'Angleur (Belgium), were an unusual centre groove profile. Trams began running on Anlaby Road and Hessle Road from 5 July 1899, and Holderness Road on 12 April, 1900.

ANLABY RD. HULL. PB 248

A main Hull depot with workshop facilities was built at Liverpool Street on the Hessle Road route and there was also a depot on Wheeler Street on the Anlaby Road route. A depot with facilities for track maintenance was on Stepney Lane (Beverley Road route) and opened in 1898. Steam trams were operated for a time on the Hedon Road route due to problems of electric trams crossing a railway line. But this was overcome in December 1903. The Spring Bank route was extended along Princes Avenue on 8 October 1903, and a service to the Pier was opened in October 1903. The Marfleet line was introduced 1903, Spring Bank West, October 1913 and Hessle Road - Pickering Park, February 1914. Each route was denoted by a letter on the front of a tram: A, Anlaby Road; B, Beverley Road; D, Dairycoates (Hessle Road); H, Holderness Road; S, Spring Bank; P, Pier; M, Marfleet; SW, Spring Bank West; DP, Hessle Road - Pickering Park. The new system eventually included nine miles of double track and a half mile of single track. Built in 1899 by Milnes, double deck, open top car no. 17 is seen in Anlaby Road. A 'short' canopy cover was fitted between 1905-9.

Above

The Hull tram system had reached its maximum extent, at 20.48 miles (32.96 km) by 1927. A number of level crossings caused delays to the trams. This was because crossings required both, catch points for the cars, and interlocking with the railway signalling system. In 1925, the Corporation, Ministry of Transport and the North Eastern Railway's successor, the London & North Eastern Railway, proposed to eliminate the level crossings at a cost of £1¼ million, but no work was done during the lifetime of the trams. In 1930 the electric power station on Osborne Street was closed; afterwards the electricity supply for the trams was purchased from the Hull City Corporation's own electricity supply. In 1931 the tram service to Victoria Pier was replaced with a motorbus service. Double deck, short top covered car no. 116, travelling along Prince's Avenue and approaching the Anlaby Road crossing, was built in 1903 by Milnes. The vehicle was initially open topped, but received a covered top before entering service.

Below

By 1903 the City Centre-Spring Bank-Princes Avenue system had been extended along Newland Avenue, the Holderness Road route extended as far as Aberdeen Street and new electric tram services to Victoria Pier and along Hedon Road had opened. Depots were constructed on the eastward Holderness and Hedon routes. In 1909 a new depot on Cottingham Road took over from the Stepney Lane depot for vehicle storage. In the 1920s further extensions were added; the Holderness Road section to Ings Road, the Anlaby Road section to Pickering Road - both on reserved track. Additionally, a line was completed from Beverley Road along Cottingham Road to its end at Hall Road, and another line constructed along Chanterlands Avenue from Spring Bank West to Cottingham Road. Double deck, short top covered car no. 28 was built by the J.G. Brill Company (Brill) in 1899.

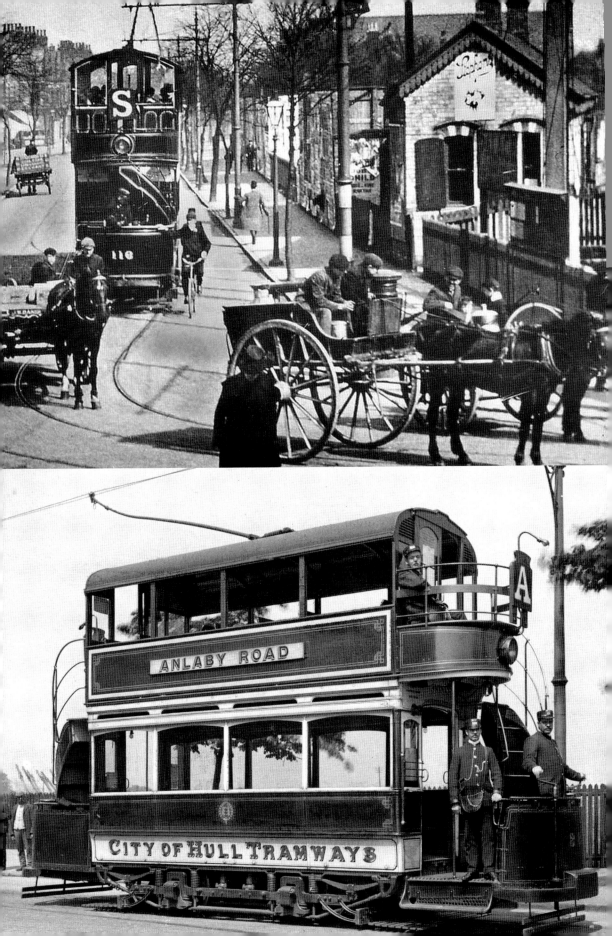

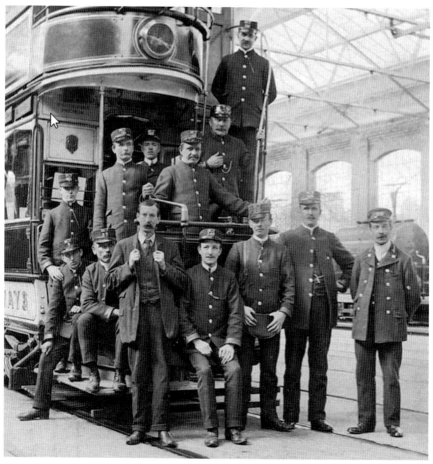

The number of Hull trams had reached its maximum of 180 and all were numbered sequentially from 1 to 180 by 1915. In 1934 the City of Hull Transport Corporation entered into a co-operation agreement with East Yorkshire Motor Services (EYMS). Thus, services were divided into three areas: Hull City, its suburbs, and the surrounding countryside. Revenues for services were split between the two companies irrespective of service provider – the city transport company received revenues from the city area, whilst EYMS received the revenues for service outside Hull, revenues in the suburbs were split between the two. As a consequence it became uneconomic to operate the outlying tram routes; services on most of the routes built in the 1920s were replaced by bus services. Double deck, short top covered car no. 33 is pictured working on the Pier route. Built by Brush in 1900 as an open top car it was in a batch given short canopy covers between 1905–9.

Opposite Above
Double deck, short top covered car no. 102 was built in 1903 by Milnes as an open topped vehicle, but a Milnes top cover was added before it entered service.

Opposite Below
Tram staff pose for the camera inside the Cottingham Road Depot.

In 1936 the construction of a trolleybus system was authorised; with the exception of the Hedon Road route, which was replaced by a motorbus service, the remaining tram routes were replaced by trolleybus operation between 1936 and 1945. The final tram (no. 169) ran on 30 June 1945; the journey along Hessle Road to the depot at Liverpool Street was celebrated by the tram being driven by Alderman Hewitt and Alderman Stark acting as conductor. The vehicle was illuminated by 800 lights and approx. 50,000 people attended the farewell event. Above, two unidentified double deck trams are seen on 18 August 1906; below, an unidentified vehicle and car no 16 are seen in Spring Bank.

Chapter 2

North Yorkshire

ARBOROUGH TRAMWAYS OPENED MAY 6TH 1904.   HAPPY BE THY SPEED.

Scarborough

Edmunson's Electricity Corporation Ltd, formed a subsidiary company, the Scarborough Tramways Company, to operate tramway system in the town. Construction began on 12 October, 1903 and it opened on Friday 6 May 1904 after an inspection by Colonel Pelham von Donop. The track was 3ft 6in. gauge and covered almost five miles. The fleet eventually numbered 28 cars. The main contractor for system's construction was the parent company, Edmundson's Electricity Corporation, and its general layout was to the design of a Mr Swinton, with a Mr Waler as consultant engineer. The power for the system was obtained from Edmundson's Electricity Corporation from their town power station off Seamer Road. The costs of construction, including an extension to the power station, was £96,000. The car depot was located off Scalby Road. Pictured near the railway station undergoing trials before the official opening of the system is double deck, open top car no. 10.

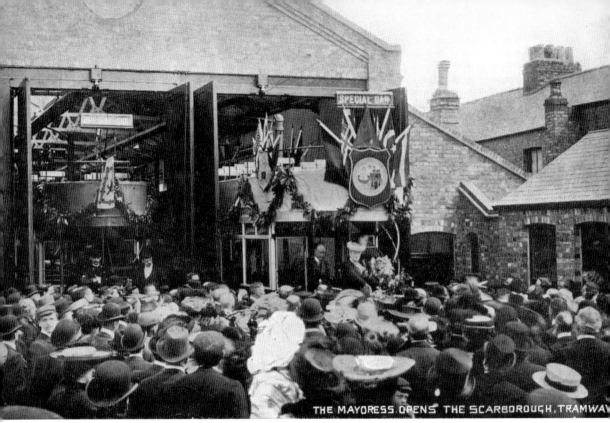

THE MAYORESS OPENS THE SCARBOROUGH TRAMWAY

Cars numbered 1-15, delivered in May 1904, were built by Brush and seating was available for 43 (20/23). Nos 16-18 arrived later in the year and nos 19-22 were delivered in 1905. H.V. Vinks, in *Tramway Review* Vol. II No. 82 Summer 1975, states that all 22 cars were built by Brush under contract to British Thomson-Houston, who supplied the electrical equipment. In 1925 a batch of six cars were purchased second hand, for £50 each, from Ipswich Corporation Tramways. These became Scarborough nos 21, and 23-28. The original no. 21 was involved in an accident yet its truck was utilised for the 'new' no. 21. Mayoress Mrs W. Morgan officially opened the Scarborough tramway system and taking part in the celebrations were thirteen cars. The run started from the Scalby Road tramshed. Cars numbered 1 and 2 are seen here. Part of an account of the opening day is recalled by Vinks (1975): 'On the appointed day cars left various central points in the town between 11.30 a.m. and 12 noon with official guests, and proceeded to the depot. Here 13 of the 15 cars were formed into a procession, their indicators reading "Special Car", and each car was decorated with orange coloured drapings and evergreen festoons. The leading car, driven by the manager Mr J.M. Edmundson, was more elaborately turned out than the rest, and carried on the front a shield with the borough coat of arms...The front of the depot was similarly festooned.' Public services on the opening day began at 3.30 p.m. and finished at 11 p.m. During that time it was estimated that approx. 6,900 passengers had used the tram services. On the following day the system boasted carrying around 10,000 people.

The Scarborough routes were as follows: Route 1, from West Pier to Scalby Road was 1.9 miles; Route 1A - Aquarium to Scalby Road, 1.7 miles; Route 2 - Aquarium to Manor Road, 2.25 miles; Route 2A - West Pier to Manor Road, 2.12 miles; Route 3 - Railway Station and North Side via Westborough, Aberdeen Walk, Castle Road and North Marine Road. 1.2 miles; Route 4 - South Sands (Marine Drive South Toll House) and North Side via Sandside, Foreshore Road, Vernon Place, Aberdeen Walk, Castle Road, and North Marine Road. 1.9 miles. The top picture shows car no. 5 moving along Foreshore Road; the one below an unidentified vehicle parked alongside the beach.

Double deck, open top, car no. 16, seen on North Marine Road, is probably working route four - South Sands (Marine Drive South Toll House) and North Side via Sandside, Foreshore Road, Vernon Place, Aberdeen Walk, Castle Road and North Marine Road. The route length was 1.9 miles. Vinks (1975) notes that in mid-summer route four operated six to eight cars, with a car every five to seven minutes and a round trip time of 40 minutes. He also mentions - as may have been predicted - in the winter, Scarborough's tramway services operated on a very restricted scale. Because of Scarborough's narrow streets, the cars were built to a restricted width of 6ft 3in. The livery was dark red with cream for the decency boards. 'Scarborough Tramways' was carried in shaded medium sized lettering. None of the Scarborough cars ever received top deck covers. The Scarborough system was closed on 30 September 1931 and taken over by the Corporation, the company accepting an offer of £19,500 with £500 towards the cost of reinstating the roads. The United Automobile Services Ltd then ran motorbuses for the Corporation on a profit sharing basis. The trams were later sold as scrap by the Corporation Engineer. Interestingly, during their lifetime the trams had run about 5¾ million miles and annually carried approx. 1¾ million passengers.

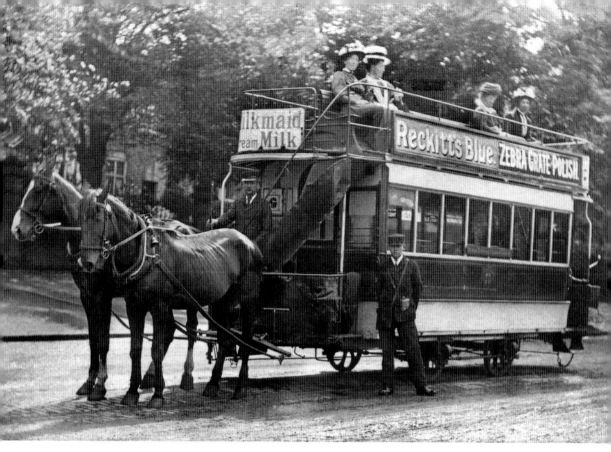

York

On 27 October 1880 the York Tramway Company's line from Castle Mills Bridge to Fulford Village was officially opened. The track was 4ft 0in. gauge with stone setts. J.F. Weston of London was the contractor and the rails were manufactured by the Darlington Iron & Steel Company. For the outward journey, to Fulford Cross, a horse tram was used and a steam car for the return one. The Starbuck Company of Birkenhead supplied three trams to open the line. They were single deck and could accommodate eighteen passengers. A further nine cars were eventually acquired. In December 1880 further routes were approved by York Council and they opened during the following year. These included a line from Castle Mills Bridge to Castlegate, and routes to the Mount and the railway passenger station. And horse trams were to be preferred over steam powered ones. Joe Murphy in *City of York Tramways* (2002) states: 'After experimental runs the [steam trams] were abandoned due to public complaints about noise and dirt. It is possible that the cars were returned to the supplier in early 1881.' By 1882 the route mileage was three miles eight chains. A double deck, open top, horse tram is pictured here at the Mount terminus. Note how underfed the first horse appears.

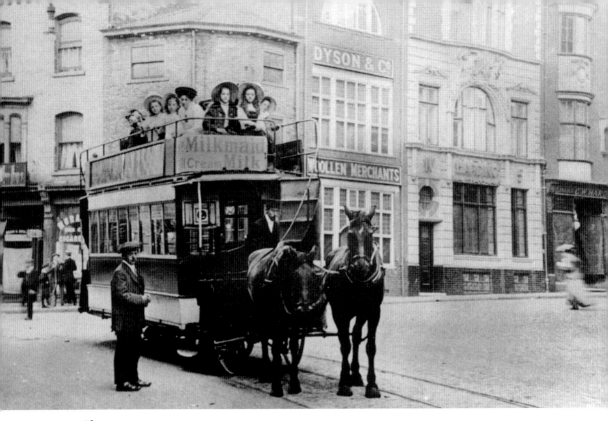

Above
The City of York Tramways Company eventually acquired the assets of the York Tramways Company for £14,500. By 1891 the company operated 10 tramcars - nine double deck and one single deck - with a stable of 37 horses. By 1902, Murphy (2002) notes 38 horses and 11 trams were owned 'and in February 1909 the Corporation acquired 23 horses and seven trams.' Pictured at the Nessgate/Coppergate junction is a double deck, open top, two horse car.

YORK'S FIRST ELECTRIC CAR

Above

For its new tramway system, York Corporation decided to adopt an overhead current collection system and a track gauge of 3ft 6ins. The British Thomson-Houston Company supplied the first 18 trams and a water sprinkler car for £10,914. The bodies, built by Brush, had an open top, open staircase with a canopy platform, and seated 48 (26/22). They were painted royal blue and cream with lining and lettered in gold. The Corporation eventually operated a fleet of 45 tramcars. York's first electric car, no. 1, ran fully decorated, at noon on 20 January 1910 from Nessgate to Fulford. It was 'driven' by the Lord Mayor Alderman Birch and driver J.A. Stewart. On that first day, 6,786 passengers travelled on the trams. Double deck, open top car no. 1 is seen here in Clifford Street.

Opposite

During 1905 repairs to the existing fleet of cars was undertaken and new ones added. The latter cars were larger than the previous ones and said to go more smoothly and with greater ease and speed. The system was taken over by York Corporation Tramways for £8,856 on 27 February 1909. The last horse car ran on 7 September 1909 and many of the vehicles were dismantled. One survived and was sold for £3 to Doncaster Corporation Tramways, to become a salt car. Passing over the River Ouse Bridge, a double deck, open top, horse tram is seen on its way to the Mount.

Left

The construction work on the new York system was carried out by Dick, Kerr & Company of Preston (Dick, Kerr) at a cost of £78,827. Car no. 7 is working the Acomb to Fulford route. Services commenced on that section on 9 June 1910. Double deck, open top car no. 7 had entered service by October 1910.

Below

Double deck, open top car no. 14, in service by October 1910, is working on a Dringhouses to Fulford service. Note the sign indicating the car is 'full'. The vehicle featured a Brush, 4 wheel, 8ft 6in. wheelbase truck; a B.T. - H. B18 controller; and B.T.- H. GE60 (2 x 25 hp) motors.

From 1915 four battery-operated buses were put into service between Heworth and Clifton. In 1917 a motorbus service was introduced between the Leeman Road Memorial and Leeman Road, then in December 1920 trolleybuses were in service from Pavement to Heworth. Double deck, open top car no. 11 is on the Fulford to Dringhouses route. To the rear is double deck, open top car no. 12. To the left is York railway station and hotel. By the mid-1920s, York was operating 15 buses, 37 trams and 4 rail-less cars.

Acquired in January 1910, double deck, open top car no. 2 is working the Fulford to Dringhouses route - a distance of 3.71 miles and which opened on 17 March 1910. The vehicle was in the batch, numbered 1-18, that were fitted with roller blinds in November 1916.

Above

Double deck, open top car no. 16 is travelling on the Haxby Road to Railway Station service. The first car ran between Haxby Road and Lendal Bridge on 14 June 1910; regular services not operating between Haxby Road to the Railway Station until August of that year. In 1914 to cope with the increasing use of the York tramway system, particularly on the Haxby Road route, by workers, four single-deck trailer cars were acquired with seating for 22 people. However, these were not used consistently until more powerful leading cars were obtained mid-way through the First World War. Also in the period of hostilities female drivers and conductresses were employed.

Opposite

Just before the First World War, York's tramway staff numbered 34 drivers and 33 conductors. Also at this time a route to Bishopthorpe Road/South Bank was put in hand (opening 30 July 1913) and an extension was planned to the Haxby route. This latter was completed and inspected on 19 January 1916. Following this extension and the construction of a route leading from Nessgate to Hull Road the system underwent no further expansion. The total route mileage was 8 miles 3 furlongs and 9 chains. Delivered in a batch of four (36-39) in 1916, double deck, open top car no. 36, is working on the Haxby Road route. Each vehicle, purchased from Brush cost £811 10s 0d and seated 52 (30/22). Note the vestibule platform and roller blind destination indicators which were a feature of trams in this batch and the ones numbered 28-31. Cars originally numbered 36-41 featured B.T.-H. GE249A (2 x 35 hp) motors.

Many of York's fleet of 45 trams were added before 1917: nos 1-18, 1910; nos 20-23, 1911, nos 24-27, 1912, nos 28-31, 1913, nos 32-35, 1914; nos 36-39, 1916; nos 40-41 1917. Murphy (2002) points out that nos 36-41 were renumbered 31-36 in 1924. No. 37, acquired in 1925, was withdrawn in 1928; a new no. 37 being acquired in 1929 along with nos. 38 and 39-41. Nos 42-45, ex-Burton-on-Trent Corporation vehicles, were delivered in 1930. Double deck, open top car no. 11, working on the Haxby Road to Dringhouses route, is at the Dringhouses' terminus.

At the entrance to Museum Gardens is double deck, open top car no. 8 working on the Railway station to Haxby Road service. The vehicle was in service by October 1910. An agreement was reached between York Corporation and the West Yorkshire Road Car Company to set up a joint undertaking to work services in 1934. Ultimately, this resulted in the abandonment of tram workings and the system was closed on Saturday 16 November 1935, with cars 1-4 forming a farewell procession. All the trams were sold for scrap to Grahamsleys Ltd.

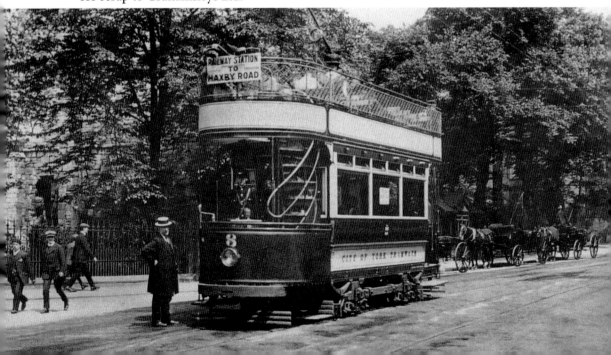

Chapter 3
South Yorkshire

Barnsley

In 1898 three companies envisaged operating tramway services in Barnsley. Barnsley Corporation itself did apply for powers to operate a rather ambitious system. All these proposals were for 3ft 6in. gauge systems. But it was a British Electric Traction subsidiary, the Barnsley & District Electric Traction Co.(BDETC), that commenced services at 3.00 pm on 31 October 1902. The takings for the first day amounted to £120 and for a time cars only ran between Eldon Street North and the two Worsborough termini. The cost of opening the lines was estimated at £58,000. Early in 1903 traffic receipts from the opening had been on average £160 per week. The BDETC tramway was a standard gauge 4ft 8½in. system and before Christmas 1902 was running from Smithies (near Monk Bretton Colliery) through the centre of Barnsley to two miles south of the town, to two termini at Worsbrough Bridge and Worsbough Dale. Double deck, short top covered car no. 8, working in Cheapside, was delivered in a batch of ten vehicles, in 1902. Built by Brush with seating for 48 (22/26), the trams originally had open tops, standard three side windows, reverse staircases, four lamps in the saloons, destination indicators above the guard rails and were painted in green and white. Other features included a Brush Type A truck, Brush 1000B 2 x 30hp motors and a Brush controller. The batch was fitted with short top covers in 1903-04, but were rebuilt with extended canopy roofs 1912-14.

Double deck, open top car no. 19, moving in Cheapside, belonged to the Yorkshire Woollen District Tramways (YWD) and ran in Barnsley during 1903-1904.

Double deck, top covered, open balcony car no. 11 is parked at the Worsbrough Bridge Terminus.

Extensions to the Barnsley system, along Park Road, Dodworth Road, Huddersfield Road and beyond Smithies were planned but never carried out. There was opposition from the Great Central Railway Company to a tramway level crossing at Worsborough Bridge and this thwarted plans to extend from there to Hoyland Nether which would also taken in Birdwell and Hoyland Common. The Barnsley fleet comprised 13 four-wheel double deck cars, a demi-car and a water car. The *Tramway Review* Vol. 7 Issue No. 52 notes that when all the BDETC's three routes were being operated a basic ten minute service was given through the town with the twenty minute service to Worsborough Bridge or Dale by each alternate tram. A separate tram shuttled the half mile between Eldon Street and Smithies. A curious observation was that the company never ran each alternate tram from Worsborough on a through service to Smithies. Double deck, short top covered car no. 8 is in May Day Green.

Double deck, short top covered car no. 10 is travelling along May Day Green. Services were operated by BDETC for colliers from 5.00am to 6.00am and later in the day for shift changes. During the first year of operation, the tramway receipts were £9,355.

Another view of car no. 10 shows the vehicle in Sheffield Road heading towards Barnsley town centre passing the drinking fountain at the junction with Corporation Street. The photograph was taken some time after 1904 when short six window top covers started to be fitted to the trams in the 1-10 and 11-12 batches. The *Tramway Review* Vol. 7 No. 52 notes that the top covers were supplied by Milnes Voss (the Magrini type) and Brush or under licence by the latter from the former. Car no. 10 is said to be the first Barnsley vehicle to receive a top cover featuring only three side windows; the others having six. The top covers cost £40 each.

Double deck, short top covered car no. 20, on loan to Barnsley from the YWD, 1903-1904, is working along Sheffield Road, Barnsley.

Double deck, open top car no. 1, on its way to Worsborough Bridge, 11 August 1905, is pictured during General Booth's motor tour. William Booth (10 April 1829–20 August 1912) was a British Methodist preacher who founded The Salvation Army and became its first General (1878–1912).

Above

Dearne District Light Railways

The Dearne District Light Railway (DDLR) was ceremoniously opened on Friday 11 July 1924. Building the line - stretching a little over 18 miles - and installing the equipment was undertaken by the Consolidated Construction Company. The track was standard 4ft 8½in. gauge. Councillors from Thurnscoe, Wombwell, Wath and Bolton - all places included on the route - attended the opening ceremony. To begin with, 12 cars set off from the Alhambra terminus in Barnsley and moved slowly to the car barns or depot on Brampton Road, Wombwell, where Mark Nokes, chairman of the DDLR, gave a speech. The depot housed six roads each one capable of accommodating five cars. The DDLR Head Office was also at Wombwell. From the depot, the cars then set out along the route and in Thurnscoe they were met by a large cheering crowd. The line from Wath to the Woodman at Swinton was not opened until September; this was in order to cope with the construction of a deviation through Burman Road, Wath. Single deck cars nos 10 and 17 are working in Doncaster Road, Goldthorpe.

Opposite Above

From 1913, the BDETC, began operating motor buses to Hoyland and other areas nearby. A name change to Yorkshire Traction Co. occurred in 1928 and the tramway system was abandoned two years later. Barnsley Traffic Superintendent Arthur Wood drives the town's last tram on 3 September 1930.

Opposite Below

Double deck, short top covered car no. 6 is parked at the Worsborough Dale terminus.

The DDLR fleet contained 30 single deck vehicles, painted maroon and cream, with gold lining. Preference was given by the company to the single deck type, on account of the limited headway under at least two of the bridges on the route. It was also argued that with the single deck car there was less oscillation and therefore greater comfort. They were built by the English Electric Co. Ltd (EEC), with 36 seats, Peckham P22 trucks, DK 30B 2 x 40hp motors and DK DB1 Form K3 controllers. The destination indicators were of the roller blind pattern and the sandboxes of the 'New Commonsense' type. The sides of the platforms were open but the fronts had glass panels. One side of the platform was fitted with folding steps and collapsible gate, but on the other side, to facilitate loading and unloading at busy traffic points, a special type of door had been designed. This was operated by the driver. The top picture shows DDLR staff alongside Car no. 3. Car no. 22 is in High Street, Wath.

The *Mexborough & Swinton Times* of 5 July 1924 gave DDLR track details: 'Mining operations are proceeding over the entire area, and special provision has been made for the possibility of subsidence by the adoption of a sleeper type of track. The foundation of the track is of handpicked stone or lump slag in large rocks and is drained by an open stone-ware pipe running along the centre of the sleepers. The sleepers are laid about 3 feet apart and the track is consolidated to within 3 inches of the rail level and completed with tarmacadam. The cost of this special form of road construction is not more than £6,500 per mile single line.' The rails and fishplates were supplied by The Cargo Fleet Iron Co.; points and crossings, Edgar Allen & Co.; road surfacing, Hadfields Ltd; installation of overhead lines, Clough, Smith & Co. Ltd; and poles, Stewart and Lloyds. The top picture shows work taking place on the track on Wombwell Lane; Car no. 17 is in Montgomery Road, Wath.

C.T. Goode in *The Dearne District Light Railways* (1997) states the DDLR cars were delivered by rail to Wombwell MR station yard, and then carted down Hough Lane to the depot, adding: 'Nos 1-25 came first, bodies and trucks separately; these were assembled by the firm's engineers at the depot. Nos 26-30 were ordered when the Woodman Inn branch was authorised.' Car no. 30 is moving along Montgomery Road, Wath.

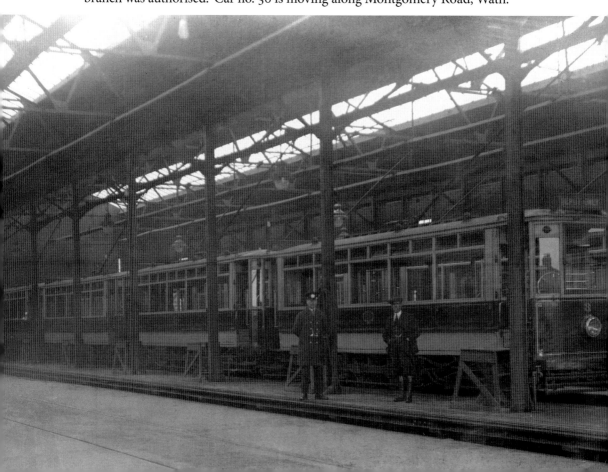

After leaving Barnsley, the DDLR route passed through Stairfoot to Wombwell, Brampton Bierlow, West Melton, West Staithes and Wath-on-Dearne where it split three ways: north east to Thurnscoe; east to Manvers and south via Burman Road to the Woodman at Swinton. As for electrical power a sub-station was erected in High Street, Wath-on-Dearne. Through this sub-station the Yorkshire Electric Power company provided a bulk supply of three-phase current at 10,000 volts for the whole system with the exception of the three miles within the Borough of Barnsley (from Aldam Bridge to Alhambra Theatre) which was worked on direct current from the Barnsley Corporation electric station. Bett and Gillham in *The Tramways of South Yorkshire and Humberside* (1980) state that four cars were reseated about 1927 with two-and-one traverse to seat 31. It is also added: 'These four, and one other, were sold after closure to Falkirk, becoming Falkirk 11, 12, 17, 18 and 19. Four were sold to Lytham St Annes as Lytham 51-54; the trucks and other equipments of the other 21 cars were sold to Hull.' Car no. 17, is travelling along High Street, Wombwell.

Opposite Below

The car sheds or 'car barns' as they were known were situated conveniently near the centre of the system in Brampton Road, Wombwell. The large single building erected to house the cars was of brick except for one side, where the possibility of extensions had been allowed for. The car shed was 173ft long, by 70ft wide, with capacity for 30 cars. The repair shop was 65ft by 45ft; the joiners shop 30ft by 45ft and there was a paint shop to take two cars in addition to smiths shops, stores mess room, offices etc. An interior view of the barn is depicted.

Goode (1997) notes that 475,876 miles were run by the DDLR trams in the first year of operation, 2,526,279 passengers carried and they paid £23,000. But with working costs at £20,000 and debts of £4,700 it was easy to see the operation was running at a loss. Car no. 13 is depicted along High Street, West Melton.

The last DDLR tram ran on Saturday night 30 September 1933. The *Mexborough & Swinton Times* of 29 September 1933 reported that the system was to be scrapped and the Yorkshire Traction Company were to substitute buses. 'This is the end of a municipal dream...it is being jettisoned because hopes and ambitions have not been realised. The promoters have made the best of a bad job and have cut their losses by selling out to their successful rivals, the Yorkshire Traction company...', said the newspaper. Car no. 6 is at the Wombwell Tram Depot.

Doncaster

Doncaster Corporation's trams first ran on Monday 2 June 1902 with services to the western outer suburbs of Balby and Hexthorpe. Centre grooved rails were chosen and copied those at Hull, but were laid in concrete. The takings on the first day (a holiday) were £43 19s 5d for the two services and 10,533 persons were carried. Routes were subsequently opened to Avenue Road, Beckett Road, Bentley, Hyde Park, Oxford Street, Race Course and Woodlands. Car no. 11 wends its way through the Market Place whilst returning from Avenue Road to the town centre terminus in Station Road.

At the outset of Doncaster's tram operations, the town centre terminus for services to the Race Course, Hexthorpe, Hyde Park, Avenue Road, Beckett Road and Oxford Street was Station Road seen here. Double deck, open top car no. 14, working on the Balby route, was re-trucked, along with car no. 7, with 7ft Peckham P22 trucks in 1921. When no. 14 was rebuilt in 1913, with a top deck cover, the destination box was mounted in the lower saloon. The vehicle was withdrawn in 1930. Trolleybus services began on the Balby route on 26 July 1931.

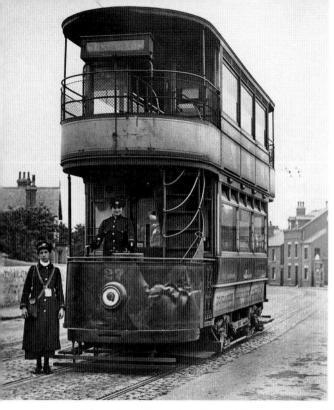

A large number of the Tramway Department's employees had left for War service by 1916 and so women drivers and conductors were employed for the first time. Female staff are pictured with Car no. 27 just west of the original Balby terminus. In *Doncaster Corporation Transport 50 Years Jubilee June 2nd, 1952* (1952) it is mentioned that during Zeppelin raids warnings were given from the Electricity station by dimming the tram lights three times successively. It also said that if power was eventually cut off oil lamps were lit whilst the trams were stationary in the streets.

The original tram terminus at the junction of High Road/Oswin Avenue, Balby is pictured here. The tracks ended in a 'Y' arrangement on either side of the tram shelter. On 5 February 1915 the Balby route was extended westwards to Warmsworth. Members of the Corporation , their wives, and invited guests, travelled by tram from the Doncaster Mansion House to Balby and along the extension to the new terminus at the Battie-Wrightson Arms public house, Warmsworth. The return journey found its way to the Electricity Station where the new extension to the building was opened on the same day. The Balby/Warmsworth tram route was closed on 25 July 1931. The route, as far as Barrel Lane, Warmsworth, was converted to trolley bus operation.

THE CAR TERMINUS BALBY

The Avenue Road and Beckett Road services were opened during 1903. Double deck, open top car no. 9 is working the Beckett Road route and is in Nether Hall Road. The Beckett Road route's outer terminus was at Morley Road. Trolleybuses began operating on the Beckett Road route from 1929.

Services commenced to Bentley on Monday 27 October 1902 - on the Bentley side of the GNR's line and a 'feeder' service was also put on from the town centre to the Marsh Gate level crossing. Passengers then walked through a subway to join the Bentley service. When the North Bridge was built Bentley trams travelled through to the town centre. Double deck, top cover, open balcony car no. 13 parked is at the first Bentley outer terminus. The Bentley route was served by trolleybuses from August 1928.

Initially, a tram shed in Greyfriars Road was built to hold twenty vehicles and four are seen here. From l to r, they are nos: 4, 5, 2 and 1. To begin services Doncaster bought fifteen cars (nos 1-15) from The Electric Railway & Tramway Carriage Works Ltd, Preston (ER&TCW) and they were open top 56 seaters (34/22) with reversed stairs, and mounted on Brill 6ft 21E trucks. All began services in June 1902. The *Doncaster Transport Official Fleet History 1902 1974* (1973) notes that nos 5-9 were fitted with top deck covers and direct staircases, by Brush in 1913, thus becoming balcony cars. Nos 10-15 were fitted with top deck covers, and direct staircases, by the ER&TCW in 1913, also becoming balcony cars. In time the Doncaster fleet numbered 47 trams, a water car and a sand and salt trailer rebuilt from a York horse car.

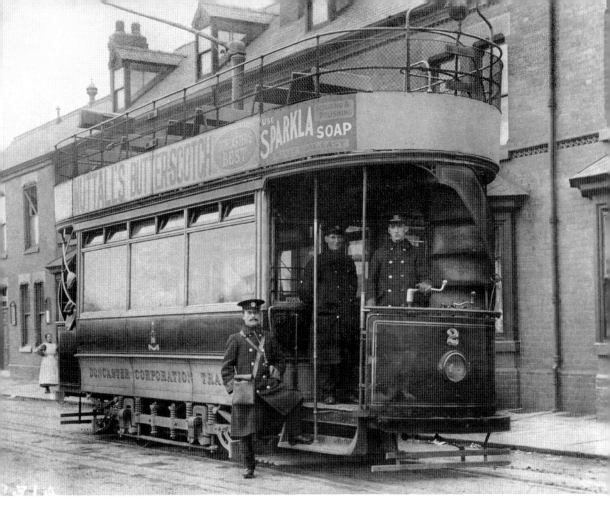

Above

The Hyde Park route was opened on 1 August 1902 to Jarratt Street and extended to Childers Street in October 1902. The route was single tracked with a 'passing loop' in Catherine Street. After the First World War plans were proposed to extend the Hyde Park service to the Racecourse, but this was not undertaken until the route was converted to trolleybus operation in 1930. Double deck, open top car no. 2 is parked at the Hyde park outer terminus near Childers Street.

Opposite

Car no. 4 is shown on what is thought to be the first trip to the Hexthorpe outer terminus. Trams were replaced by trolleybuses on the route in July 1929.

The Oxford Street service began on 25 November 1903. But, it was abandoned in April 1905 as a failure. Its revenue throughout the whole period being only £86 2s 9d. Cars are pictured along the Camden Street stretch of the route whilst picking up passengers for a local Co-op Gala.

The Brodsworth route opened during February 1916 and was mainly intended to serve Brodsworth colliery. But, the route terminated in Woodlands, seen here, and miners travelling to the colliery had to walk the remainder of the way. The Brodsworth route was the only Doncaster tram route not converted to trolleybus operation. Double deck, top covered open balcony car no. 30, was purchased in a batch of six from the United Electric Car Company Lt, Preston (UEC) in 1913.

Mexborough & Swinton Tramways Company

Opening in 1907, the Mexborough & Swinton Tramway (M&ST) used the Dolter surface-contact system, but it was converted to overhead current collection in 1908. There were 20 trams in the fleet. Nos 1-16, all double deck, open top cars, were acquired in 1906 from Brush, and seated 54 (22/32). Twelve cars were fitted with top covers in 1908 and two more four years later. Tram staff and passengers pose alongside a M&ST car at an unidentified location.

When M&ST public services commenced on 3 August 1907, every car was packed from early morning until past midnight. Double deck, open top car no. 8 passes through the narrow Mexborough main street.

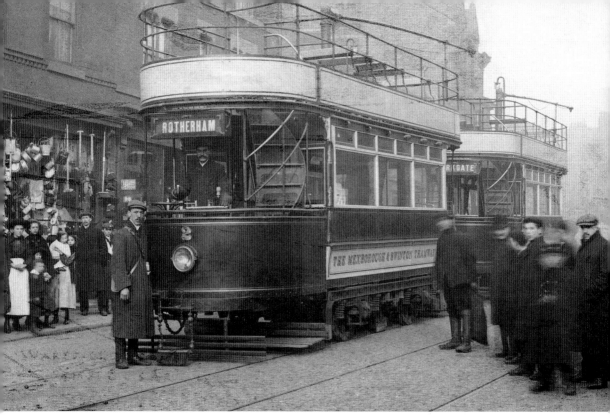

Ellis in *South Yorkshire Trams* (1996) suggests the top picture, photographed in Parkgate, with tramcars minus metal trellis around the upper decks, and a driver and conductor without uniforms 'probably depicts a trial running prior to opening.' He also adds: 'The brush, normally suspended from the rear fender, neutralised the road studs...after passing over them.' Below, double deck, open top car no. 13 is seen in Broad Street, Parkgate.

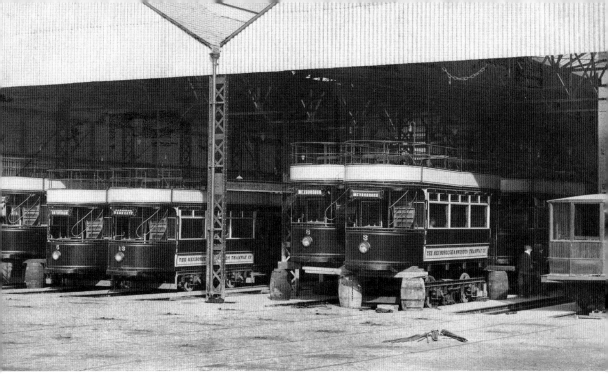

Double deck, open top cars numbered 2, 5, 13, 8 and 3 are seen in the depot at Rawmarsh, probably just before the opening of the system. The one below was perhaps taken some time later. The M&ST's line ran from Denaby to Rotherham Bridge, passing through Mexborough, Swinton, Rawmarsh and Parkgate. The lines connected to those of Rotherham Corporation at Rotherham Bridge. Powers had been obtained to run a tram line from Mexborough to Manvers Main colliery but this never occurred. Construction of the M&ST was undertaken by the National Electric Construction Company Ltd (NECC) and the first section from College Square in Rotherham to Rawmarsh Hill opened on 6 February 1907 and to the Old Toll bar at Denaby on 3 August 1907.

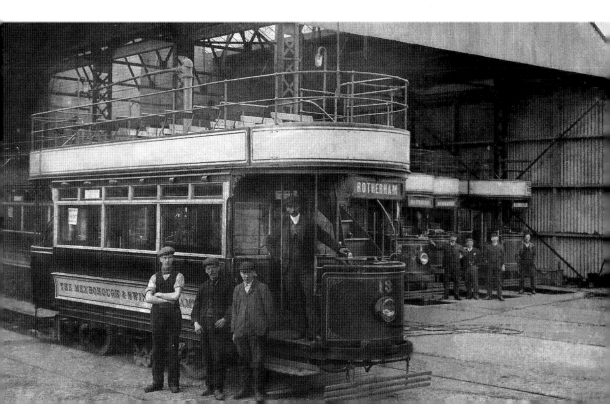

D. 5038. MEXBRO' AND SWINTON CARS.

Above
Double deck, top covered, open balcony car no. 11 is seen with a shallow and slightly domed top cover, and a side-mounted trolley boom. These features enabled this car and 11 others in the 1-16 batch to negotiate two low bridges at Rawmarsh and Swinton. The M&ST cars had a livery of dark maroon and white.

Double deck, open top car no. 13 is at Swinton Common where the Dolter surface contact studs may be seen between the rails. On straight track, the studs were placed nine feet apart, and six feet on curves. The rails were laid on concrete and infilling was with granite setts. A series of recurring incidents led to the abandonment of the Dolter system which had cost the NECC £14,000 to install. These included loud bangs and flames beneath the cars, fatal electric shocks to horses, and trams being marooned and having to be pushed along the road by passengers to regain electric power. In July 1908 Swinton UDC complained about the dangers of the Dolter system to the Board of Trade resulting in its suspension.

Opposite
Double deck top covered car no. 18, in High Street, Rawmarsh, was in a batch of four balcony cars (nos 17-20) purchased, for £2,180 each, in 1908 from Brush with 54 seats (22/32). During 1928-1929 the M&ST fleet was replaced by trolleybuses. The first section to undergo conversion was the stretch from Mexborough to the Woodman Inn which opened in November 1929.

KIMBERWORTH. F.T.

Below

Conversion from the Dolter system to overhead electrification, by August 1908, resulted in a cost of around £8,000. It should be noted that the cars were fitted with overhead trolleys from the outset for running in Rotherham. Also, three Rotherham cars were fitted with studs for workings outside their boundary. Double deck, top covered, open balcony car no. 15 passes the Don Hotel at Swinton.

29554. BRIDGE STREET, SWINTON.

Above

Rotherham

Under the Rotherham Corporation Act of 1900, Rotherham Corporation began tram services on Saturday 31 January 1903. Earlier, on Tuesday morning 29 December 1902 a trial trip had taken place from the Rawmarsh Road depot to Effingham Street and then along Fitzwilliam Road to the Pumping Station. It had been intended to open these two routes on 1 January 1903 but this failed to materialise and they were not opened until the end of January. Major Pringle inspected the track work and a Mr Totter the electrical equipment. Alderman Winter, the chairman of the Electric & Tramway Committee, officiated at the revised opening ceremony. The Rotherham lines were to the standard gauge of 4ft 8½in. McCartney, McElroy & Co. undertook work on the overhead equipment and permanent way for £7,102 and £55,419 respectively. The first services ran along the routes of the initial trial trips: from Effingham Street and terminating at the Rawmarsh tram depot; and from Fitzwilliam Road to the Pumping Station. Rotherham's first 12 cars were double deck, open top and built by the ER&TCW. They included 56 seats (22/34), 'reversed staircases', Brill 21E trucks, DK 25A 2 x 25hp motors and DK DE1 Form B controllers. The bodies had three side windows. Double deck, open top car no. 5, is pictured in a passing loop on the Kimberworth route at the junction of Psalter's Lane/Kimberworth Road. The Kimberworth route opened to the public at 3.00pm 9 April 1903.

The Rotherham tram rails were supplied by Walter Scott Ltd of Leeds; the points and crossing from Sheffield's Hadfields. Cars numbered 11 and 12 are seen in a passing loop near the Kimberworth terminus. Major Pringle in his initial inspection of the Kimberworth route stated that the single track on Kimberworth Hill should be double track. In July 1903, he returned to find the work had been done to his satisfaction.

Double deck, top covered, car no. 14 originally entered service at Rotherham in 1903 as a single deck, four wheel vehicle, seating 28 passengers. Built by the ER&TCW, it was acquired along with two other cars (13 and 15). Rotherham trams had a chocolate and yellow livery but the former was later changed to maroon. Cars 13, 14, and 15 were rebuilt by the UEC as open-canopy top-covered 70 or 72-seat double-deckers in 1908. Car no. 14, pictured on the Kimberworth route, was withdrawn by 1933.

Double deck, open top car no. 28 is at the Rawmarsh Road tram terminus with the depot seen to the rear. The depot was situated adjacent to the canal bridge at the Greasborough boundary. Charles C. Hall in *Rotherham & District Transport Vol. I - To 1914* (1996) mentions that work on the depot had commenced early in July 1902 'and was to have two sections, referred to as two sheds, one with two pairs of lines and the other with three roads. It was thought that 30 cars could be "accommodated" with a little spare space available.' Later, the depot was extended to hold 40 cars.

Rotherham car no. 21, in College Square, is ready to depart for Kimberworth. Acquired in a batch of 15 double deck, open top cars (costing £500 each) in 1903 from the ER&TCW, it was fitted with an open-canopy top-cover in 1907. Further along is Sheffield double deck, top covered car no. 174.

L.S. 172-94. College Square, Rotherham.

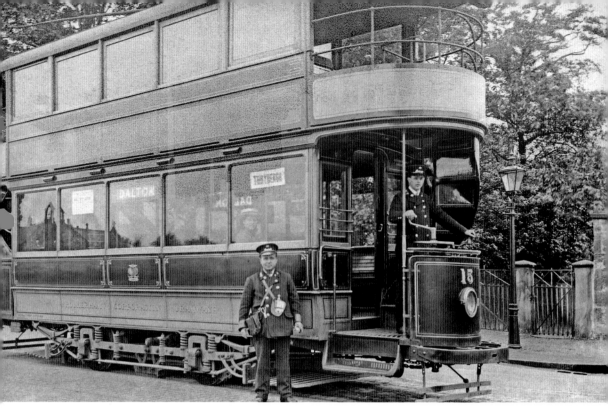

Rotherham had six tram routes: Rawmarsh Road, Broom Road, Kimberworth, Thrybergh, Canklow, and to the Sheffield boundary at Templeborough. The first four were converted to trolleybus operation in 1929, Canklow to motorbuses in 1934. Trams continued to run to Templeborough until 1949. The Fitzwilliam Road line to the Pumping Station was extended to Dalton on 1 October 1906 and further on, to Thrybergh, on 23 August 1912. Double deck, top covered, open balcony car no. 15 is seen with the route indicator showing Thrybergh.

View from Market Street and on the right is the Rotherham Corporation Tramways Water Car, no 31.

Double, deck, top covered, open balcony car no. 23 is parked in College Square. A board on the side of the vehicle reads Tinsley-Sheffield. In the distance there is a double deck, top covered Sheffield Corporation car.

Major Pringle inspected the Templeborough route on 4 June 1903 and a service from College Square to Templeborough commenced at 8.00am on 8 June. An extension from Templeborough to Tinsley was opened immediately after an inspection by Major Pringle on the afternoon of Tuesday 21 July 1903. The first service began at 5.40pm on that day. On 11 September 1905, after much wrangling between Rotherham and Sheffield Corporations, a through service came into operation. Built in 1903, double deck, open top car no. 25, pauses in College Square before working to Tinsley.

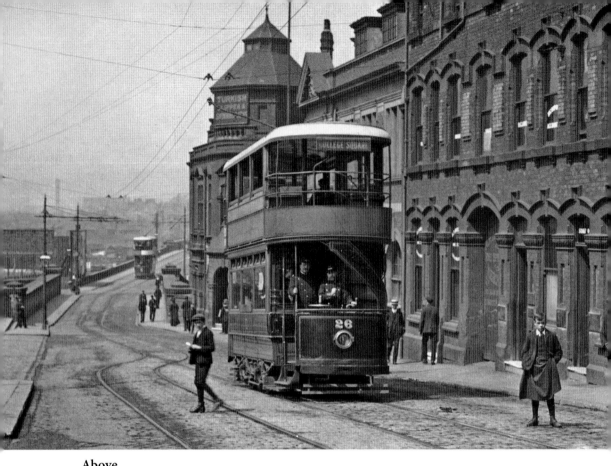

Above

Double deck car no. 26, built in 1903 as an open top vehicle, was subsequently fitted with a domed roof top cover in August 1907. The covers cost £118 each. The vehicle is working on a return journey from Kimberworth to College Square.

Sheffield

The Sheffield Tramways Act, 1872, gave the Sheffield Tramways Company (STC) authority to provide five horse drawn tramway routes. There was also a clause which permitted Sheffield Corporation to substitute themselves in place of the Company, to construct the lines and then lease them back at the annual rent of £100 per mile of route. The Corporation took up the option in August 1872. Local engineer Thomas Lightfoot of Grenoside laid the original lines and the first route from Lady's Bridge to the Golden Ball at Attercliffe was opened on 6 October 1873 and extended to Tinsley (or Carbrook) on 7 May 1874. The earliest double deck cars were quite crude, access to the roof was via an iron rung ladder and at night the saloons were illuminated by two oil lamps. But the horse trams were an improvement on horse buses and provided a smoother ride. There were depots at Nether Edge, Attercliffe, Brightside and Heeley. Double deck, open top horse car no. 33, posed on London Road, was probably built by Starbuck & Co. Birkenhead (Starbuck) in 1877 for the Heeley route (batch 32-40).

Opposite

Double deck, open top car no. 29 is travelling along West Gate with the route indication box displaying Canklow. The rails for the Canklow route were laid early in 1903 and Major Pringle arrived to inspect it on 4 June. As a result, a service between Canklow and Rawmarsh Road was started two days later. An early morning service on the route was in frequent use by Rotherham Main colliers, the pit situated a short distance from the Canklow outer terminus. The tram to the left is on the line to Templeborough. Hall (1996) notes that initially five cars were used on the Canklow route, 'the first leaving the depot at 4.30, College Square at 4.35 and reaching Canklow at 4.50.'

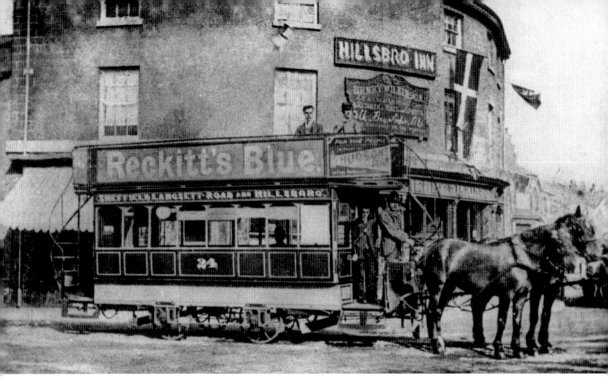

On 26 May 1875 a route was opened from Lady's Bridge to the Wellington Inn at Brightside, later extended to Brightside Bridge c. 1885. Services were established from Snig Hill to Hillsborough, 19 May 1877; Moorhead to Heeley, 29 October, 1877; and Moorhead to Nether Edge, 24 December 1877. The top picture shows horse drawn, open top, double-deck car no. 24 at Hillsborough Corner. Below, double deck, open top car no. 1 or no. 50, built 1886 by Ashbury Railway Carriages and Iron Co., Manchester (ARC&IC), is in Washington Road, Sharrow.

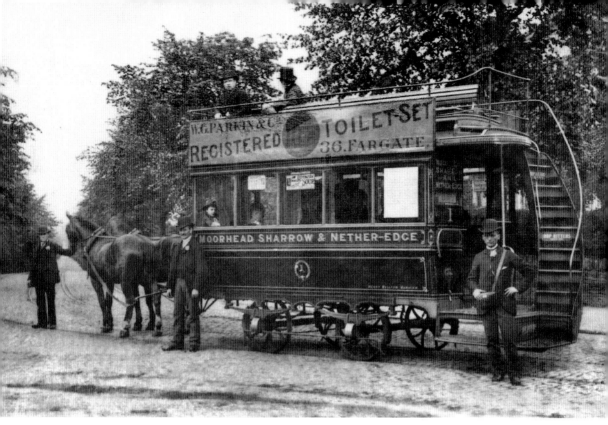

The original no. 1 car was withdrawn in 1885 and the number was taken by one of two vehicles purchased in 1886 for the Nether Edge route from ARC&IC. Pictured above, the Ashbury no. 1 double deck, open top car is parked in Moncrieffe Road facing Montgomery Road while working the Moorhead, Sharrow, Nether Edge route. Below, double deck, open top car no. 50 is at Nether Edge Terminus, Nether Edge Road.

Double deck, open top car no. 9, working on the Sheffield, Attercliffe, Tinsley route, was among the first batch of 12 double deck cars purchased from Starbuck. The photograph was taken in Tinsley Depot Yard at the time of the 'Corporation' takeover, 1896. The Corporation's first General Manager, Henry Mallyon, is the man in the foreground wearing a top hat.

Car 16, with a double deck and open top, is at The Moorhead, working a service from there to London Road and Heeley.

When Sheffield Corporation took over the system on 10 July, 1896 the fleet included 44 tramcars, 4 omnibuses, 310 horses, 9 miles of track and 182 employees. The first Corporation horse tram service operated the following day. Car no. 52 was one of four double deck, open top cars purchased by the Corporation in 1897 (nos 51-54) to work on the Nether Edge route. It seated 34, had a livery of Royal Blue and is working along High Street. In total the Corporation ran 67 horse cars, 43 double deck and 24 single deck, until the turn over to use electric cars.

In August, 1897, the Corporation planned to convert all the existing tram routes to an electric overhead system. Additionally, routes were to be constructed between Moorhead and Lady's Bridge and along Ecclesall Road to Rustings Road, the Wicker Arches to Firth Park, and Fitzalan Square to Walkley, Intake and Crookes. Thereafter to cope with the expansion new double deck horse cars were ordered as well as new electric cars. The last horse drawn tram ran on 11 November 1902. Open top, double deck car no. 28, seen in Fargate, was acquired from Milnes in a batch of 13 in 1900.

Above

On 1 October 1899 the Corporation began a horse tram service to Hunters Bar. It was converted for the use of electric trams - working from the Moor to Hunters Bar - on 13 April 1900. Routes to Hunters Bar, Banner Cross and Hangingwater Road were initially known as Eccelsall. The route was extended from the Hunters Bar/Rustlings Road junction to Banner Cross on 1 August, 1908 and to Millhouses Lane, 14 April, 1922. Displaying an Eccelsall route board, double deck, open top car no. 123 was in a batch (nos 104-123) built by Brush 1900-1901. By 1906 the average working week for tram drivers and conductors was 64 hours. Conductors were paid 5½d per hour and drivers 6¾d. From 1906 time-and-a-quarter was paid on Sundays. Staff only worked alternate Sundays until 1908 when a six-day week was introduced. The Eccelsall electric tram route closed on 27 March 1954.

Opposite

The track layout in Fitzalan Square was altered and redesigned several times during the early days of electric trams. Single deck car no. 40, acquired in a batch of twelve (nos 39-50) from Milnes in 1899, seated 28. The vehicles had Peckham Cantilever trucks and BTH GE52 2 x 25hp motors. A route destination board on no. 40 reads Pittsmoor. Between August 1913 and September 1914 the vehicle received a vestibule platform. Open top, double deck car no. 121 may be seen in the distance.

Above

The Firth Park electric tram route via Barnsley Road was opened on 27 September, 1899 from Wicker Arches to Bolsover Road. On 25 August 1909 it was extended to Firth Park (Bell House Road bottom) and on 18 November, 1934 from Firth Park to Sheffield Lane Top. The cars pictured are on Firth Park Road at the Bolsover Road terminus. Open top car no. 214 was included in a batch of six vehicles (nos 213-218) added to the fleet in 1904. Double deck, open top car no. 181 belonged to a batch of 20 cars (nos 167-186) acquired from Cravens Railway Carriage & Wagon Co. Ltd, Sheffield (Cravens) in 1902 seating 51 (22/29). Between 1903 and 1919 the car underwent two rebuilds.

The electric tramway track to Fulwood (via Broomhill) opened on 25 March, 1901, stretching from Winter Street to Manchester Road. On 1 August of the same year the route was extended to Ranmoor Post Office; on 12 October to Storth Lane and on 12 July, 1923 to Canterbury Avenue. Closure came on 22 August 1936. Double deck car no. 149, at the junction of Fulwood Road (straight ahead) and Nethergreen Road (to the right) was originally built by Milnes with an open top, entering service in 1901. The vehicle seated 51 (22/29) and a top cover had been added by 1913.

The Handsworth Road route opened on 11 April 1901 - from Staniforth Road junction to Darnall (Main Road); Darnall to Finchwell Road 29 May 1909; Finchwell Road to Orgreave Lane, 7 September, 1934. The route closed on 4 May, 1957. Double deck, car no. 13, fitted with a short top cover, is standing in front of the Norfolk Hotel at the Handsworth terminus at the Finchwell Road corner.

Double deck, vestibule, open balcony car no. 349 was built in a batch of ten (nos 346-355) by Sheffield City Tramways (SCT) in 1913 and seated 58 (22/36). Along with a number of others, car no. 349 was fitted with a new enclosed top deck from 1924. The car was photographed with the route indicator displaying 'Heeley via Queens Road.'

A busy High Street scene shows cars numbered 198 and 253 and an unidentified single deck vehicle displaying the route letter W. Track laying and erection of standards and overhead wires in the early years of the electric tramways caused much disruption in the city centre and often there were temporary closures of certain thoroughfares. Double deck, short top covered car no. 198 was built as an open top vehicle by SCT in 1903; 253 was also built at Sheffield, entering service with a short top cover in 1905.

Above

A horse tram service to Hillsborough (Holmes Lane) was opened on 19 May 1877 and ended on 11 November 1902. The Middlewood electric tramway route was started from Hoyle Street to Parkside Road on 30 May 1903, to Catch Bar Lane on 8 September, 1913 and to Middlewood on 26 November, 1913. Originally built as a double deck, open top vehicle by Cravens in 1902, car no. 168, seating 51 (22/29), has paused at Hillsborough at the junction of Parkside Road and Middlewood Road.

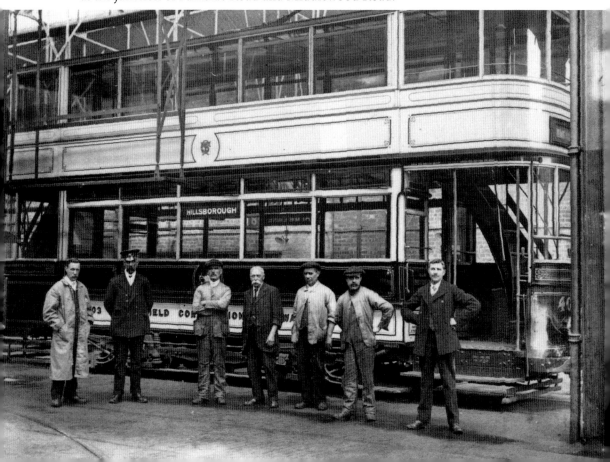

Kenneth Gandy in *Sheffield Corporation Tramways* (1985) mentions that the Corporation's initial tram destination descriptions 'in some cases were not consistent with the geographical locations concerned.' For instance 'Nether Green: Via Broomhill known as Fulwood [and] Nether Green Via Hunters Bar known as Nether Green.' The Nether Green electric tramway route was opened from The Moor to Hunters Bar, 13 April, 1900. It was extended to Hangingwater Road, 28 October, 1901 and to Nether Green, 14 May 1904. The view is facing west and cars numbered 233 and 81 have paused at the entrance to Endcliffe Park, Ecclesall Road at Hunter's Bar. No. 233, originally an open top vehicle, was built by Brush in 1904 with seating for 51 (22/29). No. 81 also began services as an open top vehicle and came from the ER&TCW in 1900, seating 51.

Opposite
Formerly belonging to the STC, the depot at Holme Lane, Hillsborough was enlarged in 1914 to comprise eight roads and accommodate 55 trams. The depot, remained in use until 1954 when cars on the Ecclesall-Middlewood route were replaced by motorbuses. Double deck, enclosed car no. 403 was built in a batch of 50 vehicles (nos 401-450) by SCT, 1919-1920.

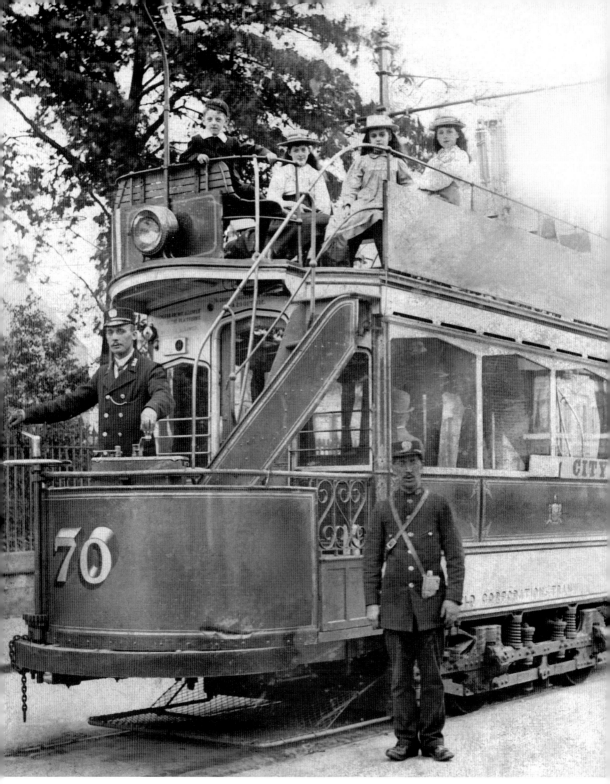

Millhouses electric tramway initially began from The Moor to Woodseats Road on 28 July, 1900 and the following extensions were made: to Bannerdale Road, 1 March 1901; Millhouses Lane, 17 April, 1902; Wagon and Horses, 31 July, 1926; Woodseats via Abbey Lane, 14 April, 1927. A note on this photograph claims, double deck, open top car no. 70, built by ER&TCW, Ltd in 1900, was the first car to Millhouses.

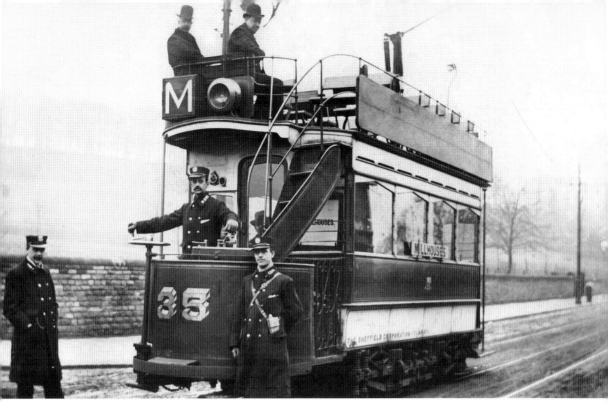

Double deck, open top car no. 35, acquired from Milnes in 1900, is located on Abbeydale Road whilst working on the Millhouses route. In 1900 Sheffield had 22 miles of track and by 1914 the system had stretched to 82 miles.

Originally built by Milnes as a double deck, open top vehicle in 1901, car no. 133 is at the Millhouses terminus on Archer Road. The railway station is at the rear. The last car ran on the Millhouses and Beauchief route on 8 October 1960. This was also the day electric tram services ceased in Sheffield. The city never operated trolley buses even though the Sheffield Corporation Act of 1912 had authorised their use.

Car no. 1 is moving along on the Moor on the first day of electric tram operation, 5 September 1899, with the Lord Mayor at the controls. He was supervised by the city's new electrical engineer, Aubrey Fell. Car no. 1 was one of twenty five, double deck, open top vehicles delivered by Milnes during the latter year. They seated 51 (22/29). In 1905 the administrative offices of the tramway undertaking were gathered together in the former Waterworks offices in Division Street and became the department's Head office.

Car no. 151 prepares to depart from Moor Head to Millhouses. Originally double deck, and open top, the vehicle dates from 1901 when it was supplied by Milnes. By March 1910 Sheffield had 264 vehicles; the total in the country as a whole was 11,123.

An unidentified open top, double deck car is at the Nether Edge tram terminus, situated at the Nether Edge Road/Machon Bank Road/Moncrieffe Road junction. A horse tram service to Nether Edge had started on 24 December 1877. The electric tram route - High Street to Nether Edge - was opened on 5 September, 1899. Closure came on 24 November, 1934.

Car no. 29 built as a double deck, open top vehicle by Milnes in 1900, is at the Nether Edge tram terminus. It is pictured before receiving a top deck cover which was fitted between 1903-1913.

Above
Running north east, the Petre Street electric tram route was opened on 24 September, 1903, extending between Fitzalan Square and Canada Street. Abandonment of the route came on 19 April, 1925. Double deck, open top car no. 113 was built by Brush 1900-1901.

Opposite
Sheffield had 69 single deck cars, like the one seen here, and they were built by a number of manufacturers including Milnes, ER&TCW, Brush, SCT and Cravens. Thirty five vehicles were sold between 1918-1920; twenty one were rebuilt as double deckers; nine were converted to snow ploughs and the same number were fitted with vestibule extended platforms. The single deck vehicles were mostly used for routes with steep inclines and low railway bridges.

Above

From 20 June 1905 rails were connected at Tinsley to those of Rotherham Corporation, but a through service did not commence until 11 September 1905. The track was doubled on the section between Tinsley and Rotherham from 25 July 1909 with the exception of a stretch under Bessemer Bridge and over the Bow Bridge, near Rotherham. Originally open top and supplied by ER&TCW, double deck, short top car no. 72 has paused in College Square, Rotherham.

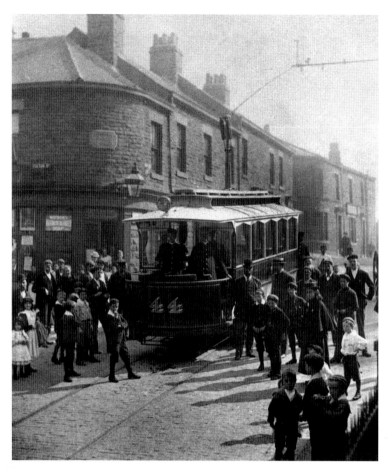

Sheffield Corporation ran horse trams to Walkley (Harcourt Road) from 7 November 1898. Extending from Church Street to South Road, the electric tram route to Walkley was opened on 18 September, 1899. Yet, the horse tram service continued for a time to Harcourt Road after electric trams were introduced. Seen on South Road, single deck car no. 44 came from Milnes in 1899 and seated 28 passengers. The Walkley tram route closed on 7 April 1956. Car no. 205, at the Walkley tram terminus, was built by SCT in 1905 and seated 28.

Chapter 4
West Yorkshire

Bradford

Bradford Corporation gained powers under the Bradford Corporation Tramways Order, 1881, to construct its own tramway system within the city. The first route ran from Rawson Square in the city centre, to Lister Park Gates. It was leased to the Bradford Tramways Company (later the Bradford Tramways and Omnibus Company Limited - BT&OC) and opened to the public on the 31st January 1882. A fleet of six horse-drawn open-top 38-seat double-deck tramcars (nos 1-6), built by Ashbury of Manchester were used. On 8 August 1882 a line was opened along Leeds Road to Stanningley and steam traction was used because of the gradients involved. In time lines to Tong Cemetery, Allerton via Four Lane Ends and an extension of the horse line from Manningley to Undercliffe were opened. In 1884 a new line was constructed from the Town Hall Square to Shelf and the Bradford and Shelf Tramways Company (B&STC) was granted a lease, expiring on the same day (31st January 1903) as those of the BT&OC. An 1896 Act removing the prohibition on local authorities operating their own tramways led Bradford Council to initiate plans to construct and operate its own system. Later, on 1st February 1902 the Corporation purchased outright, the BT&OC and the B&STC. On 31st January 1902, the horse trams that had been running on the Manningham Lane service since 1882 were finally retired. During 1903 the last steam tram ran on the former B&STC track and the Bradford tramway system became fully electrified. Steam tram no. 12, coupled to trailer car no. 38, is illustrated outside the Thornbury depot towards the end of the 19th century.

The BT&OC began a steam tram service from the city to Allerton (Reservoir Hotel) in 1883. From November 1887 the outer terminus was moved to the Druids Hotel, in 1901 an extension was made to Allerton (Ivy Lane). Steam trams ceased to run from 31 January 1902. Electric trams began on 6 June 1902 from the city to Allerton and extensions were made in October 1902, 1903, 1904. Car no. 67, at the Allerton Road/ Allerton Lane junction, was built as an open top double deck vehicle by Brush in 1901.

From 23 February 1892, steam trams from the city travelled as far as Wyke via Manchester Road, Odsal and Huddersfield Road. They were replaced by electric trams on 3 May 1902 and the route was extended to Bailiff Bridge on 17 May 1913. Double deck car no. 108, built in a batch (nos 69-128) by Brush in 1901-1902 originally had an open top. It is pictured at Bailiff Bridge outer terminus with a short top cover.

OPENING OF BINGLEY TRAMWAY,
FEB; 3RD 1914.

Left

On 3 February 1914 the Nab Wood to Bingley (Burrage House) section was opened and the celebrations amongst locals are seen here. On the day of the event three cars were involved: nos 229, 187 and 144. Car no. 229 had the Lord Mayor at the controls while car no. 187 was driven by the chairman of Bingley UDC. On 25 August 1914 the Bingley (Burrage House) to Bingley (Post Office) stretch opened and on 13 Oct 1914 the Bingley (Post Office) to Crossflatts line came into being; Bradford's last major tramway extension.

Below

The City (Tyrrel Street) was linked to Lidget Green by an electric tram service from 31 August 1900. An extension was subsequently made five years later and the route number 4 was adopted in 1919. Conversion to trolleybus operation occurred on 12 December 1934. Double deck, short top cover car no. 24, pictured at the Cemetery Road/Clayton Road junction - the Lidget Green outer terminus - entered service in 1899 and was withdrawn in 1921.

SECOND WEST HOTEL

Double deck, open top car no. 178, displaying Nab Wood on the route indicator, was delivered by Milnes in 1903. Seating was for 51 (22/29) and the vehicle was withdrawn in 1919. Nab Wood was originally part of a Mid Yorkshire Tramways Company route stretching between Nab Wood and Thackley. It was taken over by Bradford Tramways on 30 April 1904 and incorporated into the workings of their system; the Nab Wood - Saltaire section being linked to the city - Saltaire route.

Left

Electric trams operated between Manningham Lane and Lister Park Gates from 28 February 1902. The service reached Frizinghall, 8 March 1902; Branch Hotel 29 April 1902; Saltaire, 17 May 1902. On 29 May 1902 an extension of the route inward to Forster Square made a direct service from the city to Saltaire. Then, during May 1904 a link to the Undercliffe route was formed. Officials from Bradford and Shipley are amongst those pictured with double deck, open top car no. 118 on 29 April 1902 whilst inspecting the Frizinghall to Branch Hotel section. Built by Brush in 1902, the vehicle received a top cover in 1908.

Below

Electric tram services started from the city to Horton Bank Top on 27 August 1898. The route was extended to Queensbury on 2 August 1901 and was double track. The outer terminus finished close to the rails of the Halifax tramway but was not connected. Route no. 3 was allocated to the Queensbury service in 1919 and conversion to motorbus operation occurred on 5 November 1949. Open top cars nos, 40 and 33, each seating 51, were first into service in 1900 and were assembled at the Horton depot. No. 33 became an illuminated car in 1929.

On 8 August 1882 a steam tram service was commenced (Bradford's first) between Thornbury (Thornhill Terrace) via Leeds Road and the city centre. A cross city route was formed from 9 September 1882 when the Thornbury service linked with that of the Four Lane Ends route. Extensions took place in 1885 and 1887. Electric tram services began between Thornbury Depot - Stanningley on 16 November 1900; steam trams ceasing on 31 January 1902. Double deck, car no. 219, supplied by Milnes, entered service in 1903 and is pictured adjacent to the Thornbury Depot.

A service between Undercliffe and Forster Square was originally served by steam trams from 10 October 1888. Electric trams started on 28 June 1902, steam trams ceasing earlier in the year. The route was extended to Greengates on 14 October 1904 and closed on 11 Nov 1928. The city to Undercliffe route was operated by motorbuses from 7 April 1935 to 11 September 1939 until trams were used once more, lasting until 18 July 1948. Double deck, open top car no. 169, pictured in Harrogate Road, Undercliffe, was built by Milnes, entering service 1903.

OPENING OF WIBSEY TRAMWAY
OCT 9/07

The Wibsey tramway opened on 9 October 1907 extending from Tyrrell Street along Little Horton Lane, Brownroyd Hill, Fair Road to High Street, Wibsey where the picture here was taken. Cars numbered 26 and 25 took part in the opening ceremony. King (1998) says that the Black Dyke Mills Band 'played triumphal music on the open deck of car no. 25...Cars for the [Wibsey] service were provided jointly by Bowling and Horton Bank Top depots.' Wibsey tram services lasted until 8 January 1945 when converted to motorbus operation.

The trolley boom is being turned by the conductor of an unidentified double deck, short top covered top (but obviously in the 200-209 range) at the Wibsey terminus.

Electric trams operated on the Wyke route from 3 May 1902. Milnes of Birkenhead built car no. 190 in a batch (nos 129-228) in 1902-1903 and it was later fitted with a top cover. It is standing at the Wyke terminus adjacent to the new Board School on the left. Double deck, top covered car no. 193, with vestibule, is standing at the slightly resited Wyke terminus in Huddersfield Road. An alteration occurred in 1905. No. 193 is displaying the no. 14 for the Wyke route - 15 was for Bailiff Bridge. Route numbers were introduced in 1919.

Dewsbury, Batley & Birstal Tramway Company

The Dewsbury, Batley & Birstal (sic) Tramway Company (DB&BTC) completed a tramway between Dewsbury and Birstall in 1875. It was 4ft 8½in. gauge. The Dewsbury to Batley section was completed on 25 July 1874; Batley to Carlinghow on 25 March 1875 and Carlinghow to Birstall, 23 June 1875. It was extended from Birstall (Smithies) to Gomersall in 1881. A fleet of seven double deck horse trams, built by Starbuck, were originally operated on the single track route, with passing loops. Steam trams, built by Merryweather & Sons Ltd, London (Merryweather), eventually numbering eleven vehicles, and trailers (fourteen in total) from Ashbury and Brush, were introduced from 10 April 1880. They ran alongside the horse trams. This was the first on-street tramway in England. Gilham and Wiseman (1962) note the DB&BTC livery was chrome yellow, 'engines originally dark brown or black.' The DB&BTC was eventually controlled by the British Electric Traction Company (BETC) and services ceased around September 1905. New electric services were then introduced in the area by the BETC subsidiary, the YWD. DB&BTC car. no 7, built in 1881, is pictured in Northgate, Dewsbury with a double deck trailer car.

Opposite
Dewsbury, Osset & Soothill Nether Tramways
During the last week of October 1908 trial runs were made over the Dewsbury, Osset & Soothill Nether Tramways system. The name was eventually shortened to Dewsbury & Ossett (D&O). The formal opening was on Thursday afternoon 12 November 1908 and the fleet comprised twelve vehicles. Public services began on the following day. These included a main run from Dewsbury Market Place to Ossett Market Place and another between Dewsbury Market Place and Earlsheaton. The entire plans for the system were never carried out and it never underwent any extensions. The National Electric Construction Company (NECC) undertook the laying of track and construction of overhead equipment. The tramway was owned by the authorities of Dewsbury, Osset and Soothill Nether but leased to the NECC. The system, mainly single track with passing loops, was 3.125 route miles and 4.45 track miles. Open top cars nos 3 and 2, were involved with the opening of the tramway and were decorated for the occasion. Council members from the three authorities attended the event with the Mayor of Ossett, the Chairman of Soothill Nether Urban District Council and the Dewsbury Town Clerk each having spells at tram driving. Double deck, open top car no. 3, was built by Brush in 1908, and seated 54 (22/32). Later the vehicle received a balcony top cover.

Left

On 12 October 1915, double deck, open top car no. 3 - running light - left the rails at the terminus in front of Dewsbury Town Hall, crashing into Hilton's shop, adjoining the Scarborough Hotel. The driver jumped off the car ten yards before it came in contact with the building, and the conductress, Maggie Sadler, also tried to escape, but both were injured. Tuesday afternoon was a half day for Dewsbury traders and their assistants and it was fortunate there was no one on the premises or the result might have been more serious. From statements made by several eye-witnesses, it would appear that it was owing to the greasy state of the metals, through the rain, that the driver lost control of the car about 100 yards from the terminus. The front portion of the car smashed through the wall of the shop and was embedded inside it. An hour later, the room above, occupied as a drawing room and a billiard saloon, suddenly collapsed and fell on to the car and into the Market Place. Damage to the building, contents, and car was estimated between £2,000 and £3,000.

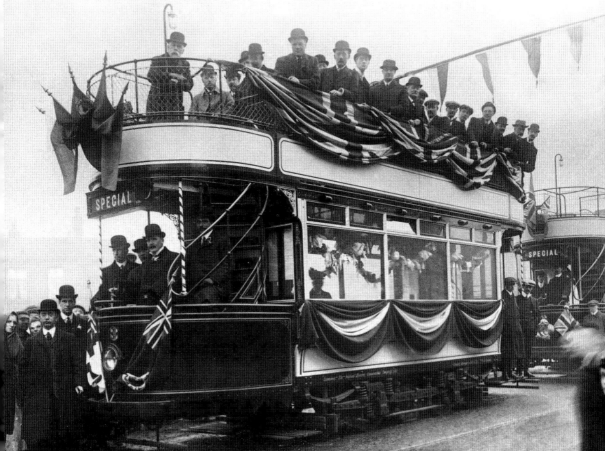

Opposite Above

Two D&O cars are seen on 26 June 1915 at the Dewsbury terminus participating in a military display. Initially the D&O car livery was dark red and off-white though this later changed to maroon and off-white. Pickles (1980) notes that the 1914-18 War period was a very critical time for the D&O. 'For its size the company had a greater percentage of men called to the colours than any other system in the country. This caused drastic curtailing of services, and in October 1917 the morning services between Dewsbury and Earlsheaton were discontinued altogether.' Yet, the number of passengers carried increased considerably after the cessation of hostilities as in 1920 the D&O recorded that 2,959,170 people had used their services. It is also worth mentioning that there were frequent protests of overcrowding on D&O cars.

Opposite Below

The D&O track was standard gauge 4ft 8½in. and the point work was undertaken by Edgar Allen & Co. Ltd of Sheffield. The company's new trams were transported from Brush by rail to Ossett railway station. Then, they were carried on low bogies to the Church Street tram shed. D&O fleet numbers 9-12 were acquired at different times from the M&ST (another NEC company); nos 9 and 10 in 1911 and 11 and 12 in 1928. All the vehicles were eventually fitted with top covers, nos 1-8 between 1915 and 1925. Double deck, open top car no. 3 arrives at the Earlsheaton Town Street tram terminus on the opening day,12 November 1908, and is welcomed by a number of residents.

Left
Car no. 6, a double deck open top vehicle, is outside the Ossett Church Street tram depot with two tram inspectors alongside. Features of cars in the batch nos 1-8 included half turn direct spiral stairs and destination boxes hung immediately beneath the canopy. The Dewsbury & Ossett Tramways Company was eventually absorbed by the YWD; the last D&O trams operated on Sunday 19 October 1933.

Halifax Tramways

Halifax Corporation operated trams officially from 9 June 1898 and for the public from 29 June 1898. Originally the livery was blue and white; a number of cars were grey 1914-18, bright red and yellow 1922-5 and dark red and white from 21 July 1921. Services radiated from the town centre to a number of areas including Queensbury, Causeway Foot, Hebden Bridge, Shelf, Brighouse, Stainland, Southowram, Skircoat Green, Triangle, Pellon, High Rd Well and Bailiff Bridge. The system eventually covered 39.07 miles. Services to Stump Cross (Staups Lane) began on 5 June 1900. Routes were later extended beyond here, north east to Shelf, south east to Brighouse and from the latter point to Bailiff Bridge. Pictured near Stump Cross and displaying a Brighouse route board, open top car no. 32 was built by Milnes and entered service in January 1899. Seating 46 (22/24), it was withdrawn in 1929. The first Halifax tramway to be abandoned was the Brighouse to Bailiff Bridge section on 30 March 1929; the Brighouse route 6 May 1931. Closure of the Halifax system started from 1931 and was completed on 14 February 1939. Brearley (1960) states that seven trams crowded with passengers made the last ceremonial trip from Masons Green, through the city centre to the depot; six trams carried the public, the last tram at 10.20 pm carried the town's officials. 'In 40½ years they had carried 820 million passengers and run 75 million miles, despite the steep hills and narrow 3ft. 6in. gauge,' said Brearley.

Opposite Below

D&O tram staff pose alongside double deck, open top car no. 2 in Church Street, Ossett. The D&O fleet numbers, placed above the headlight, were painted in gold, blocked blue and shaded black. Also in Church Street, adjacent to the car sheds was the Yorkshire Electric Power Company's sub-station from where the power for the system was generated.

A public service opened to Illingworth Post Office, 5 August 1899, and extended to Ratten Clough, 30 August 1900, stretching to Causeway Foot on 21 September 1900. The tramway route closed on 18 January 1938. Double deck, vestibule car no. 124, one of a batch of four, was built in 1931 by Halifax Corporation Tramways (HCT), seating 51 (19/32). Thornton and King (2005) note that the car was a 'De-Luxe', designed by Walter Young. Photographed at the junction of Causeway Foot and Syke Lane, it was withdrawn on 14 February 1939 and burnt in the depot yard.

A route to King Cross was opened on 29 June 1898, extensions took place to Sowerby Bridge, Wharf Street 17 October 1902 and Sowerby Bridge, Jerry Lane 21 May 1903. The tramway route closed on 29 November 1938. Car no. 79, a double deck, open top vehicle, is parked at King Cross and preparing for the return journey to the town centre. The vehicle entered service during July 1902, received a top cover in 1908, among other modifications in later years, and was withdrawn in 1937.

Open top, double deck car no. 70 built by Brush, seating 46 (22/24) entered service in the spring of 1902, received a Brush three-window canopy top in 1913 and was withdrawn in 1938. The car is standing at the King Cross terminus.

Double deck car no. 88, built by Brush as an open-top vehicle, entered service in August 1903 and seated 50 (22/28). In 1912 the same company fitted a top cover to the car and it was withdrawn in 1934. The view is looking north along Northgate to the junction with Broad Street. Several routes radiated from the Northgate/Market Street/Union Street area.

A route from the station to Boothtown (Claremount Road) was completed on 29 March 1899. It was extended to Stock's Gate, 22 December 1900, the Cavendish Inn 25 January 1901 and to Queensbury 25 April 1901. The tramway route was closed 31 March 1934. Single deck car no. 103, pictured at the Queensbury terminus, was built in 1924 by HCT, and seated 36 (later reduced to 34). Interestingly, after withdrawal in 1935, the vehicle was used, according the Thornton and King (2005), first as a retired people's shelter and then during WWII as an air raid wardens' look out post.

Pictured at the bottom of Salterhebble Hill, Huddersfield Road, with the route destination board displaying West Vale, is double deck, open top car no. 38. A route from the town to Salterhebble (Dudwell Lane) was opened on 20 January 1899 and extended to West Vale 3 August 1905. Further extensions to Holywell Green took place on 24 March 1921 and to Stainland on 14 May 1921. The tram route was closed on 30 October 1934.

Double deck car no. 92 is parked at the terminus on Skircoat Green Road. Seating 50 (22/28), the car was built as an open top vehicle by Brush in 1903, received a top cover in 1912 and rebuilt c.1922. The route to Skircoat Green (New Inn) opened to the public on 14 March 1899 was extended to Dudwell Lane 12 June 1925. The tram route closed on 31 January 1932. A depot at Skircoat was opened in 1904 to house 120 cars.

The conductor of Brush-built, double deck, open top car no. 67 poses at the Triangle terminus, whilst waiting to begin an inward journey to the town centre. A tram route to Triangle was reached in stages: to King Cross, 29 June 1998; to Sowerby Bridge Warf Street, 17 October, 1902; Sowerby Bridge Jerry Lane, 21 May 1903; to Triangle 10 February 1905. Closure came on 25 July 1934.

Standing at the Halifax terminus in Union Street, single deck car no. 105 is bound for Queensbury. It was built in 1925 by HCT, seated 36 and had, similar to car no. 103, 2 x 45hp Vickers type 307 VB motors. Thornton and King (2005) note the vehicle was in regular use on the Queensbury, Bailiff Bridge, Brighouse and Hove Edge services. After withdrawal in 1935 it became a holiday bungalow at Flamborough Head.

Car no.59 made the first run to West Vale on 3 August 1905. 'All Greetland and West Vale seemed to be gatherd there,' the press reported. Thornton and King (2005) added: 'The great gamble had succeeded. No Halifax trams ever failed to meet the challenge of Salterhebble Hill; uncomplainingly they ascended and descended in defiance of fog, rain, ice, snow and gravity.' Double deck Brush-built car no. 69, originally open top, is standing at the West Vale terminus.

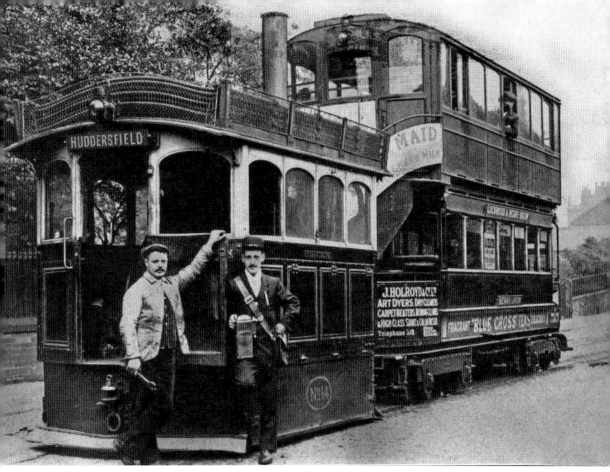

Huddersfield Tramways

Huddersfield Corporation opened its first steam tram route - between Lockwood (Red Lion Hotel) and Fartown (Royal Hotel) - on Thursday 11 January, 1883, becoming the first U.K. municipally-operated tramway system. In other towns and cities it was usual to find Corporation-owned tracks all leased to private companies. According to [Huddersfield's] *History of Undertaking 1882-1953 70 years of Operation*: 'The first ten miles of track was on the Barker system comprising a light section of rail spiked to metal chairs on a continuous bed of 7" concrete and paved with 6" stone setts...' The system was 4ft 7¾in. gauge. With the exception of the Moldgreen section the initial services were steam hauled with locomotives built by William Wilkinson & Co. Ltd (Wilkinson) and Starbuck. A former wooden circus building was converted for use as a depot in 1882, but a new building was completed in Great Northern Street in June 1887 capable of holding 30 locomotives. Larger cars were acquired from Kitsons and Greens in subsequent years, necessitating the track to be reconstructed and repaved between 1888-1893. Advertising on vehicles began in 1885 and also the carriage of parcels in 1887. In August 1896, trucks were designed for the removal of refuse and 50 tons per day were transported between a central point and a tip. An Annual report of 31 March 1897 stated the Corporation had 26 steam cars, 26 double-deck bogie cars with a track mileage of 22.16. By the turn of the century the system covered 29 miles 45 chains. The Corporation ran the last steam trams in regular service on the Almondbury and Honley routes on 17 June 1902 though several helped out with busy traffic on 21 June of the same year. Steam tram no. 14 was built in 1890 by Kitsons.

From 1885 to 1888, the Moldgreen service was worked by horse trams. Double deck, car no. 7, built by Ashbury in 1885, is pictured at the Junction Inn, Moldgreen during May 1885.

Steam trams ran to Berry Brow from 2 June 1892 and the route was electrified from 17 June 1902, when it was also extended to Honley. Double deck, open top car no. 16, working along Parkgate at Berry Brow, was in the batch of the first twenty five trams acquired from Milnes. They seated 53 (24/29), had 90 degree direct staircases and featured two BTH 35 hp GE58 motors. Painted in vermillion and cream, HUDDERSFIELD CORPORATION TRAMWAYS was seen on the panel. With the route indicator showing Sheepbridge, car no. 16 was probably working a Honley-Town-Sheepbridge service.

A steam tram route was constructed to the Peacock Inn, Leeds Road on 25 September 1891 and extended to the White Cross Inn, Bradley on 15 April 1892. Brook (1959) states that 'as the terminus here was on a hill a turning circle was provided instead of a triangle to avoid uncoupling the engine and car.' An electric tramway to Bradley was opened on Sunday 13 July 1902. An unidentified double deck, vestibule car is seen (from Colne Bridge Road) at the terminus on Leeds Road.

In a unique move, Huddersfield Corporation ran coal trains in specially designed trucks from September, 1904. This was following an agreement made with Martin, Sons & Co. Ltd, to carry all their coal requirements from Hillhouse railway sidings. It was an arrangement that was carried on until the conversion to trolley bus operation.

OPENING OF TRAMWAY SERVICE. HUDDERSFIELD TO ELLAND. - JAN.14. 1914.

A steam tram route to Edgerton was opened on 12 January 1884 and to Holly Bank (circular to Lindley) during October 1886. Becoming an electric tramway from 14 February 1901, extensions took place to Birchencliffe on 29 August 1911, Elland Town Hall 14 January 1914 and West Vale 30 May 1914. Specially decked out for the occasion, double deck, top covered car 46 is seen here on the opening of the Birchencliffe to Elland section.

An illuminated double deck, open top car decorated for the Coronation celebrations is parked outside the Tramway Depot on 22 June 1911.

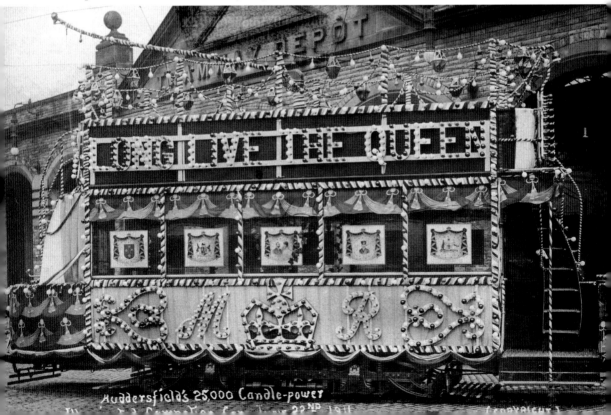

Huddersfield's 25,000 Candle-power

A double deck, open top car is seen decorated to celebrate the achievements of Huddersfield Town Football Club. FA Cup runners-up in 1920, the club won the trophy in 1922.

Double deck, open top car no. 53, displaying Bradford Road, Fartown on the route indicator, was built in 1902 by the BEC. It included three side windows, short length canopies and a direct quarter turn staircase. Seating 51 (22/29), the vehicle received a UEC short roof cover in 1912.

Double deck, open top car no. 4, entering service in 1900, is in Wasp Nest Road loop, Fartown. Steam trams operated to Birkby from 1 December 1892, and were superseded by electric trams from 6 June 1902. In the opposite direction, steam trams ran to Longwood (Quarmby Clough) from 21 May 1900, electric trams, 25 February 1901. The route was extended to Longwood (Rose & Crown), 6 July 1904, and Dod Lea 13 April 1920.

During 1914 this double deck, open top car was used as a means of appealing for recruits to join the War. As men were called up for military service, female conductors were employed until 1919 but they were not called upon to drive the trams.

HUDDERSFIELD RECRUITING CAR. 1914.

YOUR COUNTRY NEEDS YOU.

Huddersfield's electric trams first saw service on the Lindley Circular and Outlane routes from Thursday 14 February, 1901. The gauge of track used for the steam trams was retained for the operation of electric cars so that both forms of transport could be used during the transition period. The contract for the wiring of the Outlane, Lindley Circular and Slaithwaite routes was given to Greenwood & Batley of Leeds during August 1899. R.W. Blackwell & Co. were responsible for the work on the Longwood and Crossland Moor routes. Track reconstruction was undertaken by the Corporation. Services radiated from the town centre to a number of surrounding locations including Brighouse, Bradley, Waterloo, Almondbury, Newsome, Honley Crosland Moor, Marsden, Dod Lea, Outlane, West Vale and Sheepbridge. Double deck, top covered cars numbered 70 and 75 are seen here at Outlane.

A new stretch of line from Fartown Bar, and extending along Bradford Road, to Sheepbridge, was opened for steam trams on 2 April 1901. According to Brook (1959), electric cars ran from St George's Square to Fartown Bar, 19 May 1902 'extended to Sheepbridge - 20 May 1902.' Double deck, short top covered car no. 68 is at the terminus in Ash Brow Road, Sheepbridge and entered service in 1903.

A route which later ran to Waterloo initially extended as far as Mold Green from 9 May 1885 and was operated by horse trams. Steam trams first ran to Mold Green on 2 April 1888 and to Waterloo on 26 September 1890. They were replaced by electric trams from 15 May 1902. Parked on Wakefield Road at the Waterloo tram terminus is double deck car. no 34.

Keighley Tramways Company Limited

Keighley Tramways Company (KTC) constructed a horse-drawn tramway from Ingrow through the town centre to Utley in two stages in 1889. The stretch from North Street to Ingrow was opened on Wednesday 8 May; the Utley-North Street section on 18 December. The contract for the Ingrow section was given to Messrs Holmes & King of Liverpool. The Utley stretch was awarded to Messrs Winnard & Nicolls of Wigan. During 1897 short sections were added: to the Roebuck Inn at Utley and to the new Ingrow Bridge. The route was 4ft 0in. gauge, single line with loops and extended some 2.28 miles. There was a depot branching off South Street and along Queen's Road. Seven cars, supplied by Starbuck, all open top and double deck, operated on the system. These comprised four large and three small cars. The large cars could carry 44 passengers. The company sold out completely to Keighley Corporation on 21 September 1901. There had been an agreement from November 1896 where the Corporation had purchased the track for £5 and leased it back to KTC.

Above

Having bought out KTC, Keighley Corporation continued to use horse trams until 23 May 1903. Between the latter date and the start of electric traction from 12 October, 1904, the old horse route was double tracked and eventually extended to Stockbridge. Also, during this transition period Brearley (1960) notes that 'an occasional wagonette supplied the transport.' The last horse trams ran on Saturday, 28 May, 1904. Eight double deck, open top electric cars, seating 50 (22/28), were purchased from Brush in 1904 and two more in 1905. A year later two balcony cars, seating 53 (22/31) were acquired from the same company. The Keighley car livery was crimson and white. The track remained at 4ft 0in. gauge and the picture shows car no. 1 at Ingrow on 16 September on a trial run.

Opposite

Double deck, top covered, balcony car no. 8, with the destination board indicating Utley, is in Cavendish Street. The Keighley cars, nos 1-10, were fitted with Brush top covers between 1910 and 1912 amounting to £845. Gilham and Wiseman (2001) mention that Keighley Corporation 'ran Cedes-Stoll trolleybuses beyond the tram routes from 3 May 1913 until 3 May 1926.' The last trams ran on the Utley section on Wednesday 20 August 1924 being replaced by trolleybuses. The final trams ran on the Ingrow section on Wednesday 17 December 1924 and trolleybuses took over.

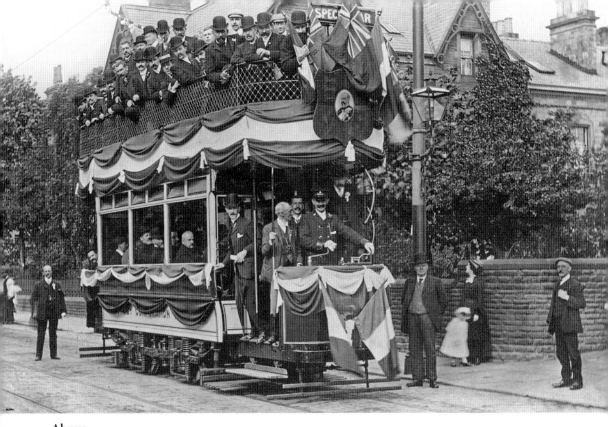

Above

A note on the reverse of this postcard states the picture depicts a group of French men on a special car near Holker Street. Marsden (2006) adds further information by speculating the men were members of a French delegation, 'presumably connected with the recent Anglo-French Entente Cordial if the portrait of King Edward VII on the front of the car is anything to go by.' It is also suggested that the gentleman with the umbrella on the front platform is Keighley Tramways Manager, John Bamber.

Car no. 8, a double deck, open top vehicle, is alongside Utley Congregational Chapel on the opening day of the electric tramways, Wednesday 12 October, 1904. Before the system was opened there was an inspection during Wednesday morning on behalf of the Board of Trade by Major W. Pringle, R.E., and A.P. Trotter, and they were accompanied by an official party. Opening to the public in the afternoon, the system carried 3,589 on the first day. The through fare from Utley to Ingrow was 1½d. A fare from Utley and Ingrow to the station was 1d.

Leeds

After much debate, between Leeds Corporation and various companies proposing to operate tramways, the Busby Brothers opened the first horse tramway route on Saturday, 16 September 1871 from the Briggate end of Boar Lane to the Oak Inn, Headingley (later extended to the Three Horse Shoes). Messrs A Speight & Sons carried out the construction work and the standard gauge 4ft. 8½in. line, extending approx. 2½ miles was operated under a lease from Leeds Corporation. The route ran from the city centre along, Park Row, Cookridge Street, Woodhouse Lane and Headingley Road, to the Oak Inn, Headingley. A route was extended from Boar Lane to the Cardigan Arms, Kirkstall Road, 1 April 1872 (eventually extended to Kirkstall village). Around August 1872 the Busby's transferred their undertaking to a new Company, the Leeds Tramway Company (LTC) working with the Continental & General Tramway Company, financial transactions being completed a year later. In July 1873 a route was opened between Boar Lane and Hyde Park; on Tuesday 3 March 1874 a route from Briggate to the Crooked Billet, Hunslet opened. Lines opened to York Road (the Woodpecker Inn) on 29 August 1874; Chapeltown on 14 November 1874; Meanwood,16 April 1878; New Wortley, 1 January 1879 (extended from 5 April 1880). The company's system eventually covered 22 miles. Horse traction ceased on 13 October 1901. The picture shows a busy scene in Briggate with three single deck horse cars visible.

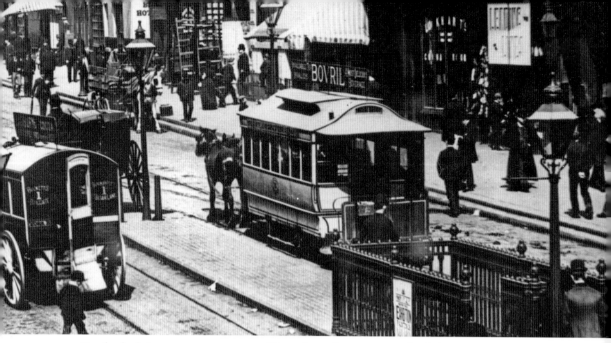

Single deck horse car no. 11, travelling along Briggate, was built by Starbuck, entering service in 1876. Initially costing £169, the vehicle seated 18.

Parked at the Queen's Arms terminus, Chapeltown c. 1890 is a double deck horse tram built by Milnes. After leaving Briggate the route extended along New Briggate, North Street, Sheepscar, Chapeltown Road, Harrogate Road to the Queen's Arms.

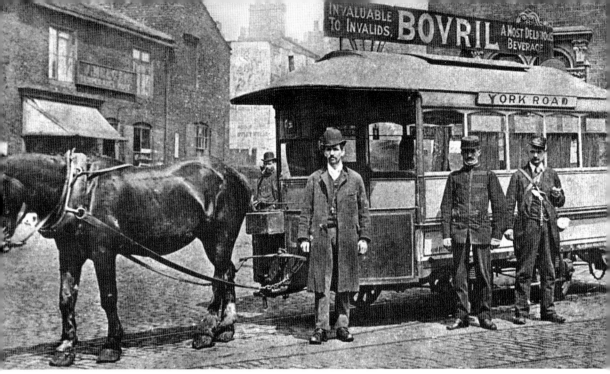

The line to York Road ran from the Boar Lane/Briggate junction, along Duncan Street, Call Lane, Marsh Lane to the terminus at the Woodpecker Inn at the Marsh Lane/ Quarry Hill/Burmantofts Street/York Road junction. Soper (1985) states that cars ran every quarter of an hour from 8.45 to 10.30pm (Saturdays 11.0pm) and the fare was 1d from Duncan Street. Horse drawn, single deck car no. 1, a 16-seater, was photographed at the Woodpecker Inn junction c.1897. Note the fork in the track layout at terminus. The vehicle was built by Milnes, seated 16 and was delicensed on 17 May 1901.

An unidentified Milnes double-deck car is seen at the Headingley Oak c. 1897.

On 18 July 1881, the Leeds Tramway Act, enabled the LTC to use steam tramcars. Kitsons supplied a large number of the tram engines along with Green. The trailer builders included Ashbury, Starbuck and Milnes. Steam traction ceased on 1 April 1902. Engine no. 28, built by Green, and trailer car no. 37, were photographed at the Wortley terminus c. 1896.

By around May 1886, the LTC was working the Headingley route entirely by steam tram cars. Pictured at Headingly are staff with Kitson engine no. 4 and Ashbury trailer no. 71. Early in March 1892, because of the track deterioration, the Company was served notice by the Corporation to stop using steam trams on the Headingley route.

Greens supplied tramway engine no. 12 in August 1885 and it was rebuilt five years later. Milnes supplied the trailer car no. 26 and both vehicles are in Wortley whilst working a service between there and Reginald Terrace. At one point during the 1880s steam trams were running every 12 minutes during the week and every 10 minutes on Saturdays on the Wortley route.

Engine no. 7, built by Kitsons, is in Wellington Street, Leeds. Costing £702, the vehicle entered service around August 1884.

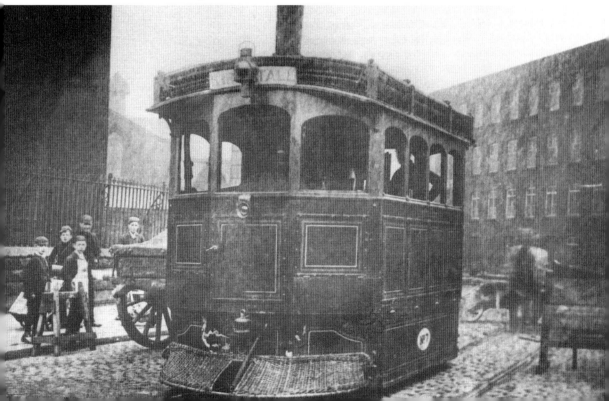

Opposite Top

The LTC's licence expired for certain routes on 14 August 1892 and the Corporation eventually took control of all the Company's assets from 2 February 1894. Immediately, matters were put in hand to repair, reconstruct and extend the track and, after much deliberation, the Corporation decided to begin operating all the tramways themselves from 1 August 1896. The Corporation's first electric tramway extending from Roundhay to Kirkstall was officially opened at 12 noon on 29 July 1897 by the Lord Mayor, Sir James Kitson, Bart, M.P. Thereafter, many new lines were opened between 1897 and 1911. Initially, the Beeston route from the city to Malvern Road was operated by horse trams from 18 July 1900. An extension was made to Beeston Police Station on 18 March 1901 and from that time the entire route was worked by electric trams. Built by Brush, double deck car no. 60 entered service between July and November 1904 and is pictured on Beeston Hill.

Opposite Bottom

Roundhay Park's opening on 19 September 1872 created a need for transport to the location. But it was not until 3 August 1889 that the first public steam tram ran to Roundhay, on track laid by Leeds Corporation. However, this was very brief and steam trams did not operate again until 15 May 1891. They were eventually superseded by the Roundhay Electric Tramway (RET), the first to be operated by an overhead wire system in Europe, and which was formally opened on Thursday, 29 October 1891. The installation was carried out by the International Thomson-Houston Company which supplied the tramcars, the overhead line and the power station plant. Steam trams ceased to operate on 10 November 1891 and the electric tramway was opened to the public on the following day. The route consisted of about two miles of double track extending along Roundhay Road, from the junction with Chapeltown Road to the entrance of the public park at Roundhay, and about half a mile of single line, running from Roundhay Road along Harehills Road to Beckett Street, where the car depot and power station had been built. The service was started up with six, single deck cars built to the designs of Messrs John Stephenson & Co. of New York and painted in a livery of chocolate and white. The tramway was leased for a period to W.S. Graff-Baker, an agent of the Thomson-Houston Company. Eventually, the tramway was also extended from Beckett Street to Kirkgate. The last Thomson-Houston car ran on the Roundhay route on 31 July 1896. Illustrated here, outside the Beckett Street Depot, is car no. 79, c. 1894.

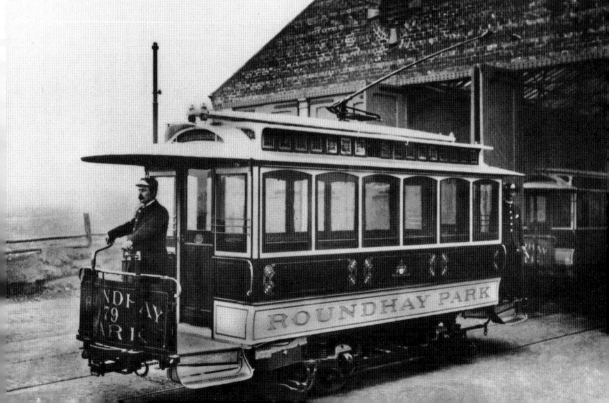

Electric trams operated to Stanningley from 2 April 1902. A branch from the latter route at Bramley Town End to Bramley Broad Lane came into operation from 14 April 1905. A further extension was made to Rodley (Bagley Lane) on 6 July 1906. Moving along Town Street, Bramley, double deck car no. 157 entered service on 24 November 1899 as an open top vehicle and seated 53 (22/31). Withdrawn on 15 December 1931 the vehicle was converted to a snow plough.

A new tramway, operated by horse cars, was opened from City Square to Cardigan Road on 18 June 1900. Electric cars started on the route from 3 August 1901. Double deck, open top car no. 170, displaying a Cardigan Road route board, was one of a number of vehicles decorated for the Royal visit on 7 July 1908.

The route to Guiseley was extended in several stages and began in April 1872 with a horse tram service to Kirkstall Police Station. An electric tram service ran between the city (Briggate) and Kirkstall Abbey from 2 August 1897. Following extensions to Horsforth and Yeadon, Guiseley (Oxford Road) was reached on 30 June 1909 and then Guiseley (White Cross) on 8 March 1915. One of the cars involved in the opening of the stretch to Guiseley Oxford Road is seen here.

A line from the York Road electric tram terminus at Halton Dial to Halton, Chapel Street was opened by car no. 311 on 30 April 1915. The route was single track with passing loops. The extension work was carried out by D. Speight & Sons. Double deck, open balcony car no. 311, with full vestibule, was built by Leeds Corporation Tramways (LCT) and entered service on 6 February 1914.

Horse cars first operated on the Headingley route from 16 September 1871, then steam trams started in June 1883. Leeds Corporation started regular electric tram services on 24 August 1899. Entering service on 30 July 1904, double deck, top covered balcony car no. 41 was fitted with a vestibule on 4 November 1912. Thus, the photograph, at Shaw Lane Headingley, was taken some time between these dates. Withdrawal occurred on 9 July 1936.

An electric line was extended approx. two miles, from Kirkstall Abbey, to Horsforth on 16 May 1906. Double deck car no. 225, made the first trip with driver C. Annakin and conductor F. Russell. The vehicle was built as an open top by ER&TCW and entered service in March 1901. Fitted with a top cover c.1904, withdrawal came in March 1927.

Horse cars operated from the city to Kirkstall Police Station from April 1872, the line being converted for use by electric trams from 2 August 1897. Pictured near Kirkstall Abbey c. 1923, is double deck, top covered, balcony, full vestibule car no. 320. It was built by LCT and entered service in April 1914. The car was in works order no. 9239 and included vehicles numbered 293-369. With a 21E truck supplied by J.G. Brill & Co., car no. 320 also had a 180 degree reversed staircase and seating for 58 (22/36).

An extension of the Headingley route from West Park to Lawnswood was completed, 18 April 1913. Soldiers from Beckett's Park Hospital are with double deck, balcony car no. 82, during the latter years of WWI. From 3 January 1917 men in uniform were allowed to travel free at specified times of the day. Car no. 82 entered service in June 1902 with a Brush open top body, the complete vehicle costing £612 11s 11d. A top deck was fitted in December 1907.

Stanningley was served by an electric tram service from 2 April 1902. A spur to Pudsey was made in 1908, Councillor Joseph Huggins, the Mayor of Pudsey drove the first car there during the formal opening on 4 June. Double deck, top covered, balcony car no. 115 was built by LCT in 1908. Seating 60 (38/22), the vehicle featured a 180 degree direct staircase and was fitted with a vestibule in May 1912.

Horse trams served a route extending along Meanwood Road to Buslingthorpe Lane from 16 July 1878. Later, steam trams were used and the route was electrified on 9 April 1900. The Ridge View Terrace, Meanwood to the Beckett Arms, Meanwood, extension was completed on 13 March 1908. Built by Brush as a double deck trailer car in 1897, no. 128 was converted to an open top, double deck car, seating 48 (28/20), and with a 90 degree direct staircase, in March 1900. Fitted with a top deck cover in May 1901, the vehicle is seen at the Beckett Arms, Meanwood terminus.

First Car LEEDS TO RODLEY, 5.30 am July 6th 1906 Conductor. W. Greenfield

A line was opened from Bramley Broad Lane to Rodley (Bagley Lane) on 9 July 1906. An inscription on this postcard view states it was taken on the opening day (wrongly noted as 6 July) at 5.30am and includes driver W. Booth and conductor W. Greenfield. Double deck, open top car no. 155, was involved in the opening run. Seating 53 (31/22), the vehicle was built with a Brush body, Peckham truck and a 90 degree direct staircase, for a total cost of £584 4s 6d. A top cover was fitted in November 1912.

A line connected the city to Thwaite Gate (Crooked Billet) from 2 March 1874 and was operated by horse cars. They were replaced by electric cars from 24 August 1900. A regular service on an extension from Thwaite Gate to Rothwell began on 1 June 1905. Double deck, top covered car, no. 64, entered service in September 1904.

Above
An electric tram service to Stanningley began on 2 April 1902. This was followed on 22 April 1907 by a through service to Bradford. Thereafter, the service stopped and started a number of times until finally ceasing in March 1918 - though cars did run to Stanningley Bottom from both cities for a number of years. Double deck car no. 279 has paused at Harrison's Avenue, Stanningley Road, Swinnow.

Mid Yorkshire Tramway Co.

The Mid-Yorkshire Tramway Co's system covered approx 3½ miles on 4ft 0in. gauge, stretching from Nab Wood, through Shipley to Thackley, and from Baildon Bridge to the Branch Hotel, Shipley. The Nab Wood to Thackley stretch opened to the public on 23 July, 1903 and cars from Bradford were used. By August 1903, the MYTC was operating its own cars. On 18 September, 1903 there was a trial run on the Baildon Bridge to Shipley section. The MYTC's fleet numbered 10 vehicles, 1-10. Built by the Motherwell firm of Hurst Nelson and Co., they were double deck, open top vehicles and accommodated 46 (22/46) passengers. Each car was powered by a 37.5 h.p. motor (type G.E.38, British Thomson-Houston Co.) and B18 controllers. The livery was royal blue, lined out in gold and white. They were housed in a shed in Exhibition Road. On 30 April 1904 the MYTC's system was transferred to Bradford Corporation. The MYTC's cars were renumbered 230-239 in the Bradford fleet.

Opposite

Electric trams ran between the city and Kirkstall Abbey from 2 August 1897. Further extensions took place including one from Horsforth (Calverley Lane) to Yeadon (Green Lane) on 26 May 1909 and the arrival of the first tram is celebrated here. Officials from the Leeds Tramways Committee and members of Rawdon and Yeadon Councils attended the ceremony. The double track line stretched approx 2½ miles.

Shipley Glen Tramway

Opening to the public on 18 May 1895 the Shipley Glen Tramway (SGT) extended 0.35 miles on 1ft 8in. gauge. Originally powered by a Suction Gas Engine, it was converted to electric in 1928. The operator was a Sam Wilson. The original stock comprised four open cars seating 12 passengers and built by S. Halliday & Son of Baildon. The SGT's website states that after a short closure, the line reopened in summer 1969 and continued until early 1981 when a right-of-way dispute prevented operations. The SGT was saved by members of the Bradford Trolleybus Association with the financial assistance of Bradford Council. Today it is under the care of the Trustees of the limited preservation company and is staffed solely by volunteers.

The Wakefield & District Light Railway Co. Ltd - later The Yorkshire (West Riding) Electric Tramways Co. Ltd

The Wakefield & District Light Railway Co. Ltd's (W&DLRC) system stretched from Sandall Magna through Wakefield towards Leeds and from Ossett to Agbrigg. It was officially opened on Monday 15 August 1904. A branch from Rothwell Haigh to Rothwell started in December 1904. Dick, Kerr & Co. Ltd (Dick, Kerr) of Preston was the main contractor for the system which was laid to a gauge of 4ft 8½ in. The main depot was at Belle Isle Wakefield, located on the Sandal route. Illustrated, on 28 April 1904, is the generating station at Belle Isle under construction. In time, the interior would house four Lancashire boilers. The WDLRC was taken over by The Yorkshire (West Riding) Electric Tramways Co. Ltd in April 1905.

Three men on a horse-drawn Dick, Kerr tower wagon are working on the overhead wiring system on Chantry Bridge. Pickles (1980) states: '[It] was suspended from 31 ft. steel poles, of which six feet were sunk into the ground and fixed in a bed of concrete... [They] were generally placed 40 yards apart. Side poles with bracket arms were the most common...the roadside poles carried ornamental scrollwork, but elsewhere they were plain.'

Work is in progress laying the track in Westagte, Wakefield. Pickles (1980) states that in constructing the track the roadway was excavated to a depth of 12½ inches, and a bed of concrete eight inches deep was then laid to carry the track and paving, this being 8ft wide for single track and 17ft wide for double track. The roadway between the rails and for 18 inches either side was paved with granite setts - for nine miles of the system. The remainder was filled with tarmacadam. The rails were laid in 45ft lengths.

In a section of the Leeds Road - between Outwood and Lofthouse Gate - cables are being laid on the eastern side.

'The vehicles are seen after arrival at Kirkgate goods yard on 25 June 1904. From there, they were transported via a temporary rail to permanent track in Kirkgate. Then, they moved to the Belle Isle depot for further assembly. The bottom picture shows car no. 24 inside the depot yard at Belle Isle. The assembly work included the fitting of the upper deck seats and mounting the trolley standards. The first 30 cars were double deck, open top, four-wheelers with three windows per side. Seating was for 56 (22/34) and the cars included 180 degree reversed stairs, and longitudinal seats inside.

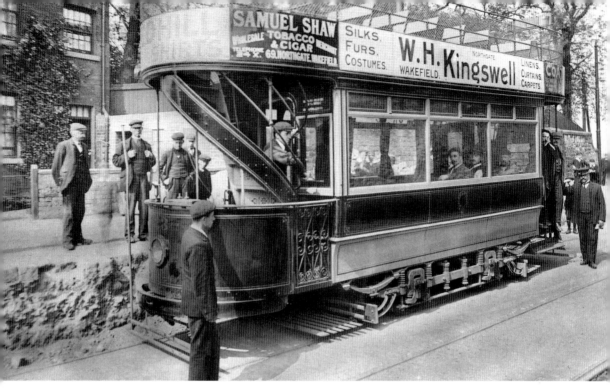

Car no. 23 is in the Belle Isle depot yard. The latter comprised five tracks and another one that gave access to the repair and paint shops. There were two smaller depots at Rothwell Haigh and Ossett. Later car no. 23 went to the detached Castleford section of the Yorkshire (West Riding Electric) Tramways Co. Ltd's system.

Whilst a caption reads 'The first car run through Wakefield', the vehicle is actually pictured in the Belle Isle depot yard. The Board of Trade inspection for the W&DLRC's system was carried out on Tuesday 9 August 1904 by Major E. Druitt, RE, and A.P. Trotter. A Board of Trade certificate was issued on 16 August 1904.

A heavy snowfall in the Horbury area during December 1906 marooned these two unidentified cars. Pickles (1980) mentions amongst the West Riding (formerly W&DLRC) rolling stock there were 'some snowplough attachments to be fitted to passenger trams.' Horbury was located on the Ossett to Agbrigg route.

Car no. 22 passes Sowood Farm and, Ellis (2004) notes, the tram staff are not wearing uniforms, suggesting 'a late 1904 date.' Initially the livery of the W&DLRC cars was crimson lake and cream. The dashes, waist panels and stairs were painted crimson lake, with lining in dark tan and orange. Above the dash lamp, the fleet number was in gold leaf, blocked and shaded. On a garter in the centre of the waist panel were the initials 'W&D. Lt. Ry. Co.'

Car no. 15 is parked at the Bank Street terminus Ossett and is about to leave for the journey to Agbrigg. It will start by turning right into Station Road. By the end of December, after 20 weeks of operation, the W&DLRC's system, had carried 1,605,221 passengers. No. 15 was in the first batch of thirty cars which arrived in 1904.

Car 22 is travelling along the single line section in the narrow Station Road, Ossett whilst on its return journey to Agbrigg. A unique feature of the car platforms was the grilles in wrought iron scroll work. Initially the W&DLRC car interiors included curtains though these were soon removed. The interior saloons were also fitted with six lamps and two oyster lights on the top deck.

Pictured on the south eastern side of the Wakefield Bull Ring, double deck, top covered, open balcony car no. 41 was built in 1905 by the ER&TCW along with nos 31-55. The vehicles had four windows per side on each deck, seated 56 (22/34), and featured half turn staircases. The electrical equipment included two DK25A 25hp motors and DK DB1 Form C controllers. The trucks were Brill 21E of 6ft 0in. wheelbase.

Double deck, top covered, open balcony car no. 39 is in Leeds Road at Outwood whilst travelling to Leeds. Ellis (2004) explains that the inconvenience of having to transfer from a W&DLRC car to a LCT car in order to reach the centre of Leeds was alleviated from 1 June 1905 onwards. The two tram operators agreed a reciprocal arrangement for through services. The Wakefield cars ran from Sandal to a terminal loop in the centre of Leeds whilst the LCT cars on the Hunslet service ran through to Rothwell.

Double deck, top covered, balcony car no. 47 is at the Sandal terminus c. 1908. Initially, the route from Sandal along Barnsley Road up to Wakefield Bridge was single track with passing loops. But from 1925, it was doubled. With the exception of a few small stretches, the main route from Wakefield to Leeds was double track.

Before the lines of the W&DLRC system were connected to LCT, passengers had to change cars at Thwaite Gate. The picture of double deck, open top car no. 25 at the junction of Wood Lane, Rothwell and the main Wakefield to Leeds road, was taken on 30 August 1904. The Rothwell Haigh depot was built nearby, containing three roads and a substation.

Open top, double deck car no. 27 is parked at the Sandal terminus outside the Castle Inn. Automatic trolley reversers were fitted at the Sandal terminus in 1916. On Tuesday 31 May 1932 the last tram operated on the Leeds to Sandal and Leeds to Rothwell routes. Traffic manager Albert Bennett drove the last car from Leeds to Wakefield. The trams were replaced by motorbuses. LCT ran to Thwaite Gate, Hunslet until 18 April 1959.

Built as a double deck, open top vehicle, car no. 9 is seen here after being fitted with a balcony top cover. The car is at the southern end of Kirkgate and about to join Doncaster Road while on its way to Agbrigg. The last trams ran on the Ossett to Agbrigg route on 25 July 1932.

Yorkshire (West Riding Electric) Tramways Co. Ltd and the detached tramway from Normanton through Castleford to Pontefract.

Having taken over the various lines of the W&DLRC, the Y(WR)TC opened a line to the public from Normanton through Castleford to Pontefract on Monday 29 October 1906. The route length was approx. eight miles and, except for a short double track sections in Oxford Street, Castleford and Pontefract, was single line with passing loops. Earlier, on 20 October the Board of Trade carried out an inspection of the system and double deck open top car no. 29 is seen on that day, entering Pontefract Road, Castleford.

A formal opening occurred on Thursday, 25 October 1906. Cars to be used on this new Castleford system were hauled from the old W&DLRC's Rothwell Haigh depot by steam traction engines. In the picture below, taken at the terminus in High Street, Normanton, an unidentified, double deck balcony car is working a tradesmen's special.

Above

A car depot at Weldon Lane, Castleford was built with four tracks to accommodate 20 vehicles. There was a power station and a paint shop adjacent, along with facilities for repairs. A fire at the depot on Monday 5 March 1917 destroyed eight of the sixteen trams housed there, along with the works car. The damage was estimated at between £10,000 and £15,000. Double deck, open top car no. 23 has passed Pontefract Park and Racecourse (and a gatehouse on the left) whilst on its way to Pontefract. Much revenue was generated for the trams when Pontefract racecourse hosted meetings.

L.L.S. 39-1. MARKET STREET, PONTEFRACT.

Yorkshire (Woollen District) Electric Tramways Co. Ltd

During the early 20th century the Yorkshire (Woollen District) Electric Tramways Co. Ltd (YWD) a subsidiary of the British Electric Traction Group, established routes, radiating from Dewsbury, and they largely fed the Spen Valley's 'Heavy Woollen District'. This included Thornhill, Ravensthorpe, Heckmondwike, Batley, Liversedge, Hightown, Moorend and Birkenshaw. Standard 4ft 8½in. gauge was used and the permanent way and overhead equipment contractors were Dick, Kerr. Initially, the YWD had an operational dispute with Batley Corporation but this was solved after much wrangling when the former agreed to lease track and vehicles from the latter. There was a circular route within Batley and it linked with Halifax Road and Bradford Road, opening on 26 October 1903. Double deck, open top car no. 54 was one of a batch of eight vehicles leased from Batley Corporation. Built in 1903 by the British Electric Car Co. Ltd (BEC), with electrical equipment supplied Westinghouse Electric Company Ltd, car no. 54 seated 55 (22/23) and was fitted with a balcony top cover in 1908. The Batley cars had a livery of green and cream, lined out, and they mostly worked in and around the town. Car no. 54 is passing the George Inn, High Street, Batley whilst working from Batley Market Place to Heckmondwike.

Opposite Below

During WWI conductresses were employed from around November 1915 and female car cleaners from about August 1916. The depleted fleet of cars lost in the depot fire was augmented by cars from Belle Isle, Wakefield and LCT. Then, in 1920, eight new cars were acquired from English Electric of Preston (EE). Double deck, top covered, balcony car no. 37 is parked at the Market Place terminus in Pontefract. Having been a loss making venture for a number of years, the system ran its last car, no. 13, from Pontefract on Sunday 1 November 1925.

PROVIDENCE PLACE
CLECKHEATON

Because of the dispute with Batley Corporation the route from Dewsbury to Moor End was opened in sections, one of them being the stretch from Quarry Inn, Staincliffe, to Moor End, on 24 April 1903. From 29 July 1903, cars operated fully along the route. Extensions from Liversedge to Hightown and Birkenshaw were opened on 28 July and 13 October 1903 respectively. Double deck, open top car no. 27 (top picture) is travelling along Providence Place, Bradford Road, Cleckheaton. Double deck, open top car no. 28 is also in Bradford Road. Both cars were in the batch 7-48, built 1902-03 and featured 90 degree reverse stairs. Originally, the YWD livery was crimson lake and cream, both lined out and the fleet number repeated on either side of the headlight.

BRADFORD RD.
CLECKHEATON.

The area on the western side of Dewsbury Market Place was used by the YWD trams. Initially, this comprised two tracks but was later increased to three. The Market Place's eastern side was used by cars belonging to the D&O. Double deck, open top cars, nos 8 and 32 have the short top covers fitted 'within' the top decks. They are about to leave for Thornhill and Cleckheaton respectively.

Double deck, open top car no. 44 is probably working an inspection 'special' while passing the Gomersal Hilltop school on 2 October 1903. The official opening took place on 13 October. Pickles (1980) points out that suggestions were made by members of the Gomersal U.D.C. regarding speed limits in the village, 'due to the nearness of the school to the tram route.' Cars from Dewsbury passed through Gomersal on their way to Birkenshaw.

The stretch from Dewsbury to the Shoulder of Mutton, Halifax Road (the Batley boundary) was opened on 18 April 1903 and from Liversedge to Hightown, 29 July 1903. Single deck car. no 55 passes through Heckmondwike Market Place whilst working a service to Hightown. There was a passing loop on the south side of the double track as it passed through the Market Place as may be seen here. Car no. 55 was originally no. 60 and built by Brush in 1904. Seating was for 20 passengers. After a collision to double deck car no. 55 in January 1904, the number was swapped with car. no 60. The vehicle belonged to batch nos 60-65 and they worked mainly on the Heckmondwike - Hightown and Cleckheaton - Moorend routes.

Another view of single deck car no. 55 (formerly no. 60) at the junction in Heckmondwike where High Street/Batley Road/Halifax Road converge. The vehicle is on its way to Batley Market Place.

NEW TRAM STA

Double deck, open top car no. 37, with Hightown on the route indicator, is in front of the YWD's Frost Hill, Liversedge, tram depot sometime in 1903. Built by Messrs Sam Drake & Garforth Bros, the shed comprised ten tracks, one of which was divided into two. During the following year, Frost Hill depot was provided with a paint shop and a repair bay.

Single deck car no. 64 is parked at Hightown Heights terminus. The vehicle belonged to the batch numbered 60-65, built by Brush in 1904, had four windows per side and was fitted with two Raworth 17hp motors, and two Raworth controllers. Also, note the brake staff outside the dash. Later, twelve single deck cars were purchased from Sheffield and worked in the Batley area as well as the Heckmondwike - Hightown service. Being redundant, some of the YWD single deck cars, after being unsuccessfully offered for sale, were rebuilt in 1924-25 into two long cars (nos 55 and 61), seating 36 inside on longitudinal seats.

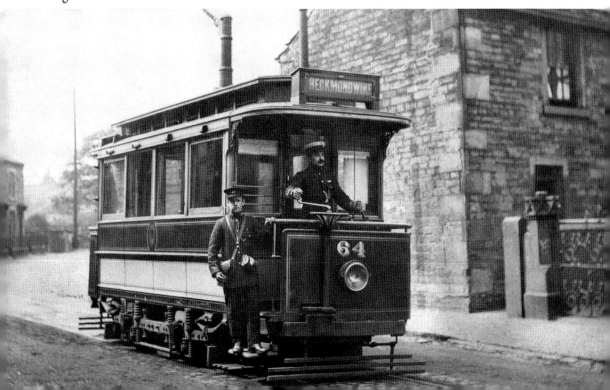

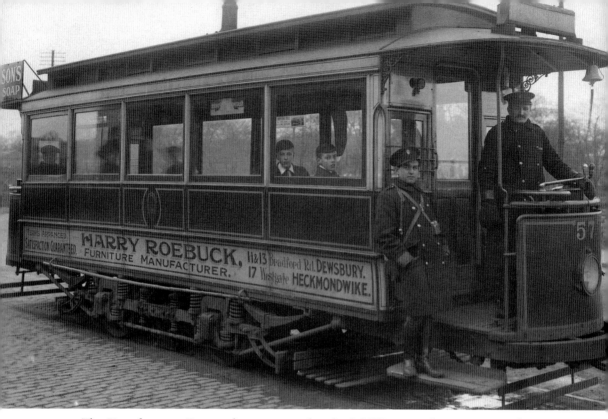

The Dewsbury to Ravensthorpe route (to the L&YR station) was inspected on 18 February 1903 and opened on 15 March 1903. An extension from the station to Fir Cottage terminus was inspected on 28 July 1903 and opened a day later. Single deck car no. 57 was one of two vehicles acquired from Brush in 1903, and seated 30 passengers.

Two unidentified double deck, top covered cars are seen crossing over the River Calder via Dewsbury's Savile Bridge whilst on their way to Thornhill. The route across the bridge, was double track. Although, the car numbers are not visible the vehicles fall into the batch numbered 7-48 and include the early type of short top covers that were fitted.

Inspected and opened on the same day, 18 February 1903, the YWD's first tram route extended from Dewsbury, through Savile Town and Thornhill Lees to Thornhill. In the top picture work is taking place on the track in Brewery Lane, Thornhill Lees. Below, double deck, top covered, car no. 18 was built by Brush - originally as an open top vehicle, 1902-03 - and seated 48 (22/26). Running with two Brush 1002A motors, each one of 32hp, the vehicle was amongst of a number that received a top cover in 1908 built by William Rouse & Son of Heckmondwike. Closure of the YWD system occurred on 31 October 1934.

Bibliography

Bett and Gillham *The Tramways of South Yorkshire and Humberside* (1980)

Brearley, H. *Tramways in West Yorkshire* (1960)

Brook, R. *The Tramways of Huddersfield* (1959)

Doncaster Corporation Transport 50 Years Jubilee June 2nd, 1952 (1952)

Doncaster Transport Official Fleet History 1902 1974 (1973)

Ellis, N. *South Yorkshire Trams* (1996)

Ellis, N. *Trams Around Dewsbury & Wakefield* (2004)

Gandy, K. *Sheffield Corporation Tramways* (1985)

Gilham, J.C. and Wiseman, R.J.S. *The Tramways of West Yorkshire* (1962)

Goode, C.T. *The Dearne District Light Railways* (1997)

Hall, C.C. *Rotherham & District Transport Vol. I - To 1914* (1996)

[Huddersfield's] History of Undertaking 1882-1953 70 Years of Operation

Hull Trams The Early Days (1977)

Marsden, B.M. *Keighley Tramways and Trolleybuses* (2006)

King, J.S. *Bradford Corporation Tramways* (1998)

Murphy, J. *City of York Tramways* (2002)

Pickles, W. *The Tramways of Dewsbury and Wakefield* (1980)

Soper, J. *Leeds Transport Volume One 1830 - 1902* (1985)

Thornton, E. and King, S. *Halifax Corporation Tramways* (2005)

Tramway Review Vol. 7 Issue No. 52

Vinks, H.V. *Tramway Review* Vol. II No. 82 Summer 1975